ILLUSTRATED GUIDE TO

ANCIENT M

in the ownership

The Minist

Volume VI

SCOTLAND

BY

the late Professor V. GORDON CHILDE, D.Litt., D.Sc., F.B.A.

sometime Professor of Archaeology and Director of the Institute of Archaeology in the University of London

AND

W. DOUGLAS SIMPSON, O.B.E., M.A., D.Litt., LL.D., F.S.A., F.S.A. Scot., Hon. F.R.I.A.S.

Librarian, The University, Aberdeen

EDINBURGH

HER MAJESTY'S STATIONERY OFFICE

1961

Published by
HER MAJESTY'S STATIONERY OFFICE

To be purchased from
13A Castle Street, Edinburgh 2
York House, Kingsway, London W.C.2
423 Oxford Street, London W.1
109 St. Mary Street, Cardiff
39 King Street, Manchester 2
50 Fairfax Street, Bristol 1
2 Edmund Street, Birmingham 3
80 Chichester Street, Belfast
or through any bookseller

Price 7*s*. 6*d*. net

First published 1952
Fourth edition 1961

CONTENTS

NOTE

The Physical Background, Prehistoric Periods, and Dark Ages by the late Professor V. Gordon Childe.

The Roman Occupation, the Celtic Period and the Middle Ages by Dr. W. Douglas Simpson.

This series of Guides to Ancient Monuments in the care of the Ministry of Works has been planned to cover England, Wales and Scotland in six volumes.

Vol. I Northern England
Vol. II Southern England
Vol. III East Anglia and Midlands
Vol. IV South Wales
Vol. V North Wales
Vol. VI Scotland

GLOSSARY

AMBULATORY	Covered walk or walk round within a building.
APSE	Circular or polygonal termination of a chancel, chapel or aisle.
ASHLAR	Dressed, squared, masonry.
AUMBRY	Small cupboard within thickness of wall.
BARMKIN	Fortified enclosure (Scottish).
BARBICAN	Forework for the defence of a castle entrance.
BROACH SPIRE ..	A type of spire which rises from the sides of its tower without a parapet.
CELLARIUM	Western range of a monastic establishment; containing stores and cellars.
CAP-HOUSE	Small chamber at the top of a wheel or spiral stair leading to the open wall-walk of a tower.
CHI-RHO	The first two letters of the Greek word for Christ—"the anointed;" used as a sacred monogram in Early Christian times, becoming common in the second quarter of the fourth century.
CORBEL	A projecting stone for the support of a timber beam or overhanging wall.
DONJON	The strongest tower of a medieval castle.
DORTER	Monastic dormitory.
ENCEINTE	Fortified enclosure.
ENTABLATURE	In architecture; the upper part of the classical orders; the architrave, frieze and cornice.
FOSSED CIRCLE ..	Earth-work or standing-stone circle surrounded by a fosse or ditch.
FRATER	Refectory: the monastic dining hall.
GARTH	The cloister garth: the cloister garden.
GROIN VAULT ..	A Gothic vault without ribs.
GUN-LOOP	Aperture for gun barrel.
HAMMER-BEAM ROOF	A type of massive open timber roof.
MORAINE	Débris deposited by a glacier.
MOTTE	A mound, partly or wholly artificial, upon which a timber castle and palisade was erected in Norman times.
PEND	Vaulted passage (Scottish).
PENNANULAR	Forming an incomplete circle.
PILASTER BUTTRESS ..	Buttress with slight projection.
PLEASANCE	Walled garden of mansion or castle (Scottish).
PORTCULLIS	Iron grille raised and lowered in grooves to defend a castle entrance.
PULPITUM	Stone screen across east end of nave of church.
QUERN	Hand-mill for grinding corn.
RAVELIN	In fortification; a detached triangular defence-work.

GLOSSARY—*continued*

RIB-VAULT	A Gothic vault with a structural framework of stone ribs.
ROOD SCREEN ..	A wood or stone screen between nave and choir on which was a "rood" or crucifix.
RUNES	An alphabetical script used by the Vikings.
SACRAMENT HOUSE ..	A cupboard or aumbry in a church; used for the reservation of the Host.
SOLAR	An upper hall in a medieval castle or manor-house.
SQUINCH ARCH ..	An arch built across an angle.
TRACERY	Ornamental stone-work in the upper part of Gothic windows.
TRANSEPTS	The northern and southern projecting arms of a cross-shaped medieval church.
TRIBUNE	Dais for a bishop's throne in the apse of a church.
TROMPES	See Squinch Arch.
TUMULUS	Burial mound.
UNICAMERAL	Single-chambered.
VOUSSUIR	An arch stone.
YETT	Open iron-work hinged gate or grille (Scottish).
THE PALAEOLITHIC (OLD STONE) AGE	Begins about 500,000 B.C.
MESOLITHIC (MIDDLE STONE) AGE	Begins about 6,000 B.C.; Britain becomes an island.
NEOLITHIC (NEW STONE) AGE	Begins about 2,000 B.C. in Scotland.
EARLY BRONZE AGE ..	Begins about 1,800 B.C. "Beaker" folk invasions; first general use of metal.
MIDDLE BRONZE AGE	Begins about 1,500 B.C.
LATE BRONZE AGE ..	Begins about 1,000 B.C.
IRON AGE	Begins in Scotland, about second century B.C. and continues into the Early Christian era.
ROMAN OCCUPATION OF SCOTLAND	Approximately 80 A.D. until end of second century.
THE "DARK AGES" ..	Approximately fifth-eleventh centuries A.D.
EARLY CHRISTIAN PERIOD ..	Approximately fifth-eleventh centuries A.D.
THE MIDDLE AGES ..	Approximately eleventh-sixteenth centuries A.D.
ROMANESQUE OR NORMAN ARCHITECTURE	Approximately twelfth century.
GOTHIC ARCHITECTURE	Approximately thirteenth-fifteenth centuries.
"DECORATED" STYLE	A Gothic style of the fourteenth century.
"FLAMBOYANT" STYLE	Late Gothic style characterised by flame-like curves in window tracery.

THE KELTS: Iron Age invaders who imposed their culture on Britain in successive waves of invasion beginning about 600 B.C.; usually spelt Celts but here spelt with a "K" to avoid confusion with *The Celts* of early Christian times in Scotland and Ireland: similarly *Keltic* and *Celtic*.

LIST OF ILLUSTRATIONS

Foreword to the First Edition

BY THE MINISTER OF WORKS

I WELCOME the opportunity of contributing a Foreword to this, the first comprehensive Guide to the Ancient Monuments of Scotland under the care of the Ministry of Works. This Guide is one of a series covering all parts of Great Britain by authoritative and distinguished writers.

Scotland is particularly rich in prehistoric remains; these are dealt with in the first part of this book by Professor V. Gordon Childe. They comprise Stone Age, Bronze Age and Iron Age dwellings; Stone Age Chambered Burial Cairns; Bronze Age Ritual Standing Stones and Rock Carvings, and Iron Age Brochs, Earthworks and "Souterrains" or "Earth Houses."

Scotland has also a varied heritage from historic times described in this book by Dr. W. Douglas Simpson. These monuments include Early Christian or Celtic Monastic Sites and Sculptured Stones: Viking Settlements, a Christian Norse Chapel, Medieval Abbeys, Castles, and Sculptured Stones; and later domestic buildings with remarkable painted walls and ceilings.

During the past 40 years the Ministry has assumed custody of a great number of these Monuments and has been responsible for their preservation and display. The Ministry has, in addition, undertaken and sponsored important archaeological excavations. It is very gratifying to record that the work of the Ministry and those associated with it has earned world-wide recognition. The Ancient Monuments of Scotland are indeed objects of interest and admiration to an ever increasing number of visitors from all parts of the world, and the Scottish public have every right to regard them with pride.

DAVID ECCLES

February, 1952

THE PHYSICAL BACKGROUND

To appreciate fully the monuments described in this guide, it is helpful not only to have some idea of their relation to the general structure of the country, but also to be able to reconstruct a landscape very different from what meets the visitor today. Scotland belongs to the Highland Zone of Britain as defined by Sir Cyril Fox. That means not so much that it is a mountainous region, which is obvious, as that it is composed of geologically ancient rocks. One consequence is a general tendency to acidity or lime-hunger in the soils. Hence the "recent moraines" left by the latest advances of the ice—notably in Aberdeenshire and Moray—the shelly sands of raised beaches all round the coasts, and limestone areas, where this tendency was naturally corrected, were especially favoured by farmers in days before artificial fertilizers or even marling were available.

But Scotland itself is traditionally divided into the Highlands and the Lowlands. The former area is geologically defined by the Great Fault that runs very roughly from the mouth of the Clyde to Stonehaven. North and west of that line the country is in fact particularly accidented and rugged, divided up by high ranges, precipitous valleys and long sea inlets or firths. A considerable proportion is too high or too wet to be habitable. Yet the Highlands comprise fertile glens, long but narrow, and even quite extensive plains round the Moray Firth and in the extreme north. But these habitable tracts are mutually isolated by lofty ridges and by firths. Hence, till the era of engineered roads after 1745, communication was far easier by sea than by land. Indeed a not inconsiderable part of the Highlands and some of the most fertile tracts are actually islands. On the west these islands, together with peninsulas like Kintyre, screen from the fury of Atlantic storms channels like the Sound of Mull and the Minch, and Firths like the Clyde and Loch Fyne for safe "inland" navigation. But they are open as much or more to voyagers coming from Ireland as to those sailing up from south-western Scotland or England. Relations between the West Highlands and the sister island have naturally been close in prehistoric as well as in historic times.

South of the Midland Valley, the broad isthmus of low-lying land between the Forth and Clyde, Galloway reproduces many of the distinctive features of the Highlands proper. But the rest of the Southern Uplands in which the Clyde, the Annan and the Tweed have their sources, though rising in places over 2,000 feet, consist of rounded hills deeply dissected by narrow fertile valleys.

So on the West, save in central Ayrshire, hills or mountains rise steeply from the sea, leaving only narrow cultivable tracts on raised beach platforms and at the mouths of straths. Habitation is naturally restricted to these isolated strips, and the equally isolated bottoms of the glens. Broader plains front the North Sea and that not only in the Lowlands proper—the Tweed basin, the Lothians, Fife and Strathmore—but beyond in Aberdeenshire, Moray, the Black Isle, Caithness and the Orkney Islands. It is here that non-industrial settlement is most extensive and intensive. But these eastern plains are mutually separated by the Lammermuirs, the Firths of Forth and Tay, the Sidlaws, the Mounth, and the Cabrach, the Beauly and Dornoch Firths, the Ord range, and the stormy channel termed the Pentland Firth.

In the past these physiographical obstacles to settlement and intercourse were supplemented by forest and marsh. Till cheap iron tools were available for tree-felling and drainage, these were just as serious barriers as mountains and seas. The grassy hills or bare moors that are now so conspicuous are only recent, and in many cases artificial products. Dense pine woods once covered even the Orkneys and climbed to over 2,000 feet in the Central Highlands. In Shetland, Orkney and Caithness these were indeed blown down over 6,000 years ago, but the rest of Scotland was still heavily wooded at the dawn of history. Gradually the random or deliberate intervention of man and of his stock had consumed or destroyed this timber till the Forestry Commission began its great schemes of re-afforestation.

In modern times coal, and, still more recently water-power, have been major factors in determining the distribution of population. In prehistoric and even medieval times these resources exercised no such attraction, but other mineral resources were appreciated earlier. For a whole prehistoric "age" copper or bronze, an alloy of copper and tin, was the sole metal used industrially by man. At that time even the smallest copper lode would be worth exploiting. Small deposits of the metal in fact existed in Galloway, along Loch Fyne and further north in the West Highlands and even in Shetland. Finally it should be remembered that game, wild fowl, seals and whales, fish, molluscs and even nuts afforded a really vital contribution to the food supply of prehistoric man.

Within this diversified region a specially large number of the prehistoric monuments to be described are concentrated in two districts—around Loch Crinan and the Kilmartin valley, and in the Orkney Islands. For these concentrations there are geographical reasons.

Plate 1. *The prehistoric village, Skara Brae, Orkney*

Plate 2. *The main thoroughfare, Skara Brae, Orkney*

Plate 3. *Stone furnishings, Hut 7, Skara Brae, Orkney*

Plate 4. *Ring of Brogar, Stenness, Orkney*

Plate 5. *Entrance to Maes Howe, Orkney*

Plate 6. *Burial Chamber and blocking stone, Maes Howe, Orkney*

The isthmus between Loch Gilp (a branch of Loch Fyne) and Loch Crinan is a natural route whereby sea-borne traffic from the Firth of Clyde and the Irish Sea could be continued after a short porterage along the sheltered waters of the Firth of Lorne. (Early navigators particularly feared rounding exposed capes like the Mull of Kintyre, and even today the Crinan Canal is useful to low-powered coasting vessels). Moreover natural trackways run up the Kilmartin valley from Crinan and thence not only to Loch Melfort but also up Loch Awe to Strath Fillan and so down the Tay system to the east coast. Between Crinan and Kilmartin extensive tracts of raised beach platform afford good arable land and pasture, the value of which is enhanced by many limestone outcrops. Finally just west of Kilmartin there are veins of copper ore, actually exploited last century and doubtless much richer before prehistoric miners worked out the superficial outcrops.

The Orkney Islands owed their attractiveness to their very treelessness. Very early the Atlantic gales had blown down the pinewoods leaving undulating grasslands and heaths admirably suited for the grazing of cattle and sheep. Peculiarities of the local rock—the Caithness flagstone and other members of the Old Red Sandstone series—partly compensate for the lack of timber. It breaks easily along its bedding planes into flat slabs ideally adapted for dry-stone building; indeed, conveniently shaped blocks, already quarried and dressed by the waves, can be collected along the shore. Moreover, some beds in the series readily yield thin slabs that can be treated as planks and are still so employed. The land is generally undulating and low-lying. The highest point on Mainland is only 600 feet, but Rousay rises in a series of terraces to just over 800 feet. Despite the high latitude and persistent high winds the climate is relatively mild. The sheltered sounds between the islands provide natural waterways. As a base for fishing and sealing and also for piracy and trade the archipelago is well situated. Seasonal winds facilitate voyages to and from Scandinavia on the one hand and Ireland on the other, and any seafarer who wished to avoid the English Channel must make a port of call in Orkney on a voyage between Atlantic and North Sea coasts. Hence the islands are exposed to influences from several quarters that are in fact reflected in their monuments.

PREHISTORIC PERIODS

THE EARLIER STONE AGE

The long period of time before written records were kept is divided by prehistoric archæologists into three consecutive stages, rather misleadingly termed the Stone, Bronze, and Iron Ages, in accordance with the material used for the principal cutting implements. In Scotland and many other parts of the Old World it has been found that stone, copper or bronze, and iron succeeded one another for that purpose always in the same order. But while there was a real period of time when bronze but no iron was employed here for axes, knives, daggers and spears, it does not follow that the Bronze Age of Scotland was contemporary with the period thus designated in Egypt or even in southern England. Nor yet were stone axes and knives abandoned as soon as copper and bronze were available. Cutting implements of stone and bone were in fact still used in the Iron Age and are not unknown in the Hebrides even today.

The Stone Age lasted much longer than the other two stages. Indeed, it comprises 95 per cent. of the whole of human history. It has accordingly been divided into two parts—the Old Stone, or Palæolithic, and the New Stone, or Neolithic, Ages, with a third subdivision termed Mesolithic rather precariously inserted between them.

The Old Stone Age coincides with the geological Pleistocene, and the last Ice Ages in high latitudes. During this period men lived with extinct animals like the mammoth and the woolly rhinoceros in Southern England and elsewhere, but Scotland was uninhabitable, being covered with ice most of the time. Only when the glaciers had melted—that caused a general rise in sea-level responsible for the raised beach already mentioned—did small bands of colonists begin to filter in from the south. All were in the Mesolithic Stage of culture: they knew no metals and practised no agriculture nor animal husbandry, but lived by collecting, hunting and fishing. Some groups have left remains of their repasts along the ancient strand, from which the sea has subsequently receded, near Oban, on Oronsay and round Loch Sunart. On the east coast relics of similar strand-loopers have been found near skeletons of whales, stranded in former estuaries of the Firths of Forth and Tay, for instance at Meiklewood, west of Stirling. Still other bands are known only from tiny flint implements or microliths collected on sandy soils in Ayrshire, in the valleys of the Tweed, the Tay and the Dee and even in Caithness and Orkney.

It is useless to speculate on the number or antiquity of these Mesolithic immigrants. The population that could find a livelihood in Scotland with a mesolithic equipment must have been inconceivably small—reckoned in hundreds, not thousands. Yet they may have contributed appreciably to the make-up of the Scottish people, since succeeding bands of colonists also were at first numerically very few.

THE NEOLITHIC AGE

The next archæological period is distinguished from the mesolithic by an economic and technical revolution that transformed the participant societies from food-gatherers, dependent for a livelihood on nature's bounty, into farmers controlling in some measure their own food-supply. It depended upon the cultivation of barley and wheat and the breeding of cows, pigs and sheep. That did not begin in Scotland, where there were no wild sheep to tame nor wild cereals to cultivate. Farming in fact began somewhere in the Near East and perhaps 7,000 years ago. Thence the arts of husbandry together with actual cultivated plants and domestic stock were slowly spread, partly at least by physical migrations of farmers with their stock and kit. They brought other arts too—pottery, textiles, improved techniques in housebuilding, carpentry and navigation.

This spread of neolithic culture must have been exceedingly slow. A conventional date for the arrival of the first farmers in southern England is 2500 B.C. The colonization of Scotland must have begun appreciably later. It was effected by various routes and by diverse bands distinguished most obviously by fashions in pottery. Some colonists certainly arrived by sea and landed at various points on our west coasts from Galloway to Orkney and even Shetland. These have left imposing monuments—great family tombs locally termed Chambered Cairns; the habitations of the living are still unidentified.

These tombs, in plan and in the ritual performed in them, belong to a large class conventionally and inaccurately designated megalithic (from Greek *μέγας* great, and *λίθος* a stone) scattered thickly along the North Sea coasts from Jutland to Holland and along the Atlantic in Eire, Scilly, Brittany, and the Iberian Peninsula and thence along the Mediterranean to Cyprus and Syria. Some of these tombs, notably in Denmark, Holland, Brittany and Portugal are really built of gigantic undressed stones and literally deserve the epithet "megalithic." But others of the same plan are constructed of more modest slabs laid in horizontal courses but naturally without mortar (dry stone masonry) while a number are not built at all, but cut in the rock.

The most important Scottish tombs are constructed of dry masonry though often combined with quite large uprights (orthostats) and cover-slabs (lintels). Like most other megalithic tombs, they were designed, like family vaults today, to contain successive burials and are therefore provided with a portal, giving access to the actual burial chamber. All built tombs were artificially put underground by covering them with a tumulus or barrow of earth or a cairn of stones. The covering mound is never a mere heap. It was always given a regular shape and defined by a kerb of upright stones or posts or a built wall of slabs or sods. Complete excavations have shown that the site of the monument was very carefully prepared and that elaborate rites accompanied its erection. They show too that, though great care was bestowed on the construction of the portal and the kerb, both features were deliberately buried in the stones or earth of the mound. They were in fact primarily ritual features. But of course it would be quite easy for the initiated to uncover the entrance on the occasion of another funeral.

The chambered cairns of Scotland can be divided into several classes by the shapes of the mound and plans of the chambers. Most in south-western Scotland—near the coasts of the Solway and the Clyde—are covered by long cairns. Such measure 90 feet to 100 feet in length and some 40 feet in width and are disproportionately large for the chambers that scarcely exceed 20 feet in length. The latter generally open on to a semi-circular space, defined by uprights at the south or east end of the mound. So these structures are known as horned cairns. The chamber itself is long and narrow, the side walls being framed of large slabs on edge which may support dry masonry corbelling inwards to narrow the space to be covered by the roof-lintels. A chamber of this plan is termed a long cist. Round the Clyde (including Kintyre and Islay) the cists are generally "segmented"—that is, they are divided into from two to four compartments by low slabs on edge (septal stones), set athwart the chamber but not reaching to its roof.

Segmented cists covered by horned cairns are common also in Nothern Ireland and on Man. Analogies are known as far away as Provence and Sardinia; so it has been guessed that the idea and presumably the ancestors of its first Scottish exponents came from that quarter. In any case the simple, leathery-looking pottery vases and leaf-shaped arrow heads of flint recovered from our segmented cists are significantly like those recovered from comparable tombs in Ulster. Already a single culture ruled on both sides of the North Channel.

That sometimes tempestuous sea, like the Aegean, united rather than divided peoples.

But chambered cairns were used for burials over several generations. Accordingly some segmented cists contain, in addition to the vases and arrow heads proper to their Neolithic builders, also Beakers, characteristic of the earliest Bronze Age, and sometimes even later Bronze Age vases and ornaments.

Nether Largie South Cairn is a fine, but not altogether typical, example of the Clyde type of segmented cist. The cairn which abnormally is round, stands beside the public road close to Kilmartin school, and is the southernmost of a line of cairns along the route already mentioned up the Kilmartin valley. It was opened by Canon Greenwell some 70 years before it was taken under the Ministry's guardianship. In the interval of neglect the cairn had continued to be pillaged for stones, the masonry walls had partly caved in, and some of the lintels had collapsed. The chamber is 20 feet long and was divided into four segments by septal slabs. Its end is still closed by a gigantic slab 7 feet high, 2 feet 8 inches wide and 6 inches thick.

In the chamber Greenwell found masses of burnt human bones in disorder and parts of at least two unburnt skeletons. The original furniture included a beautiful Neolithic bowl, now in the National Museum, but the latest interments were accompanied by Beakers of the Early Bronze Age. Outside the chamber two secondary burials, each enclosed in a short cist or coffin of slabs, had been inserted in the cairn. One was accompanied by a richly decorated Food Vessel, appropriate to the second phase of the Bronze Age. Only one cist is still exposed.

Most of the chambered tumuli in northern Scotland cover what are termed "passage graves": the burial chamber proper is preceded by a passage, lower and narrower than the chamber. Such, but with some very notable exceptions, are normally covered by round or oval cairns or barrows. In Caithness and Orkney the chambers are generally oval and built of local flagstone coursed in dry masonry technique and roofed by corbelling, but the skeleton of the building is provided in one class at least by flat slabs on end. These uprights are set in pairs projecting from the chamber walls at right angles to its main axis and so provide a portal and divide the chamber into a series of compartments, while a single slab forms the rear wall. In Caithness there are seldom more than three compartments in the chamber, but in Orkney this number is often exceeded while raised shelves or benches are generally contrived between the paired uprights along each side, to serve as the actual repositories for the corpses.

A fine and characteristic series of Orcadian tombs has been excavated on Rousay, all but one by the late Walter G. Grant, between 1933 and 1939. Most stand on the very edge of one of the terraces, so as to be conspicuous from the coastal terrace below, where their builders presumably had their fields. Each corresponds to a natural unit of settlement or hamlet with a stream, a patch of arable below the tomb and pasture above it. Four are now under the Ministry's guardianship.

Mid Howe exceptionally stands right on the shore. The oval barrow is 106 feet long and 42 feet 6 inches wide. It is supported by three concentric casing walls, each probably carried up progressively higher than the one outside it, so that the monument's exterior rose in a series of steps or stages. The same staged construction has been observed in several other Orkney barrows and has also been reported from south-east Spain. The slabs of the retaining walls are not all laid horizontally; some are set obliquely to produce decorative patterns.

The mound contains a chamber 76 feet long and over 7 feet wide, divided into 12 compartments by pairs of tall uprights projecting from the side walls. Horizontal slabs laid between these uprights and against the rear slab form benches, on which were found lying in some disorder bones from 25 skeletons. The roof had collapsed before excavation. Some uprights attain a height of 7 feet 6 inches, but those beyond the seventh compartment from the entrance on the south-east have all been broken off square some 5 feet above the ground. It looks as if there had once been a second storey here, entered from the north-west end of the mound over the truncated end slab.

Only a few shreds of pottery, some limpet shells and stags' antlers survived from the original burial furniture. The whole monument is now under cover of a "museum" building erected over it.

The Knowe of Yarso. Following the coast road eastward, the visitor would pass four chambered cairns before reaching a point directly below the farm of Yarso. The tumulus stands on the edge of a small cliff about 300 feet above sea level. It is similar in construction to Mid Howe, but much smaller. It covers a "stalled" chamber, like the foregoing, but only 24 feet long and divided by paired uprights into but three compartments or stalls. Yet it housed parts of 21 human skeletons, and bones of red deer, sheep and a dog.

Blackhammer, a little further east and standing on a lower terrace close to the road, is a mound 72 feet 6 inches long, bounded by an exceptionally well-preserved and decorative retaining wall. The chamber is 42 feet 6 inches long and divided into seven compartments in the usual way. But the entrance passage is not, as in all previous examples, at the end, but on the south side. It was found carefully blocked with stones, and the aperture through the casing wall was so well masked, that it could not be recognized from the outside. Only two bodies were discovered in the chamber, but with them was a stone axe-head, a flint knife and a handsome pottery bowl.

Taversöe Tuick stands on a flat terrace overlooking Trumland Burn, and must have been just visible from the top of Blackhammer when that mound was intact. The ruined mound was largely removed and the lower burial chamber discovered by General Burroughs in 1898 in the course of making a garden look-out, but the monument was restored by the Ministry in 1937, when additional features were discovered. The mound, now largely replaced by a concrete dome, covers two separate chambers, one above the other. The upper was much disturbed in 1898, but its general plan is clear. A long narrow passage leads from the north into an oval chamber divided by piers and measuring 15 feet 6 inches long. The floor is formed by the lintels that roof the intact lower chamber. Some of the original lintels, being broken, have been replaced, and a trapdoor inserted, to give access to the lower chamber.

The latter was erected in an excavation in the hillside which doubtless also served as a quarry, so that the rear wall is founded on ledges of rock and partly backed up against rock. From this wall project three slabs, so as to form two stalls and at the ends two "cells", all being benched as usual. There are upright slabs in the south wall, too, but these do not project beyond its line. Through this wall runs a passage 19 feet long, to the exterior of the cairn. From its inner end the passage contracts till it is only 2 feet high and 17 inches wide where it debouches from the (outer) retaining wall of the tumulus. But even beyond this point the passage was continued by a covered channel through which a ghost, but no living man, could crawl.

Just where this channel or "ghost passage" fades out, is the portal of a miniature chamber, now closed by a trapdoor. The chamber is cut in the rock, but it is lined with beautiful masonry of tiny slabs and provided with the usual projecting uprights on a proportionately diminutive scale. This chamber is about 5 feet long, 3 feet wide and less than 3 feet high. Any human bones deposited in it would inevitably be dissolved by acid waters, but it contained two miniature bowls, one decorated in the same style as those from the main lower chamber, when opened in 1938.

Three human skeletons and more than six highly ornamented pottery bowls were found in 1898, while in the passage outside lay part of a granite hammer of Bronze Age type. Cists on the floor of the upper chamber are reported to have held pottery and cremated bones, while beads of slatey stone were recovered in 1937.

Onston or Unstan on Mainland is a nearly circular tumulus on the shores of Loch Stenness close to the Bridge of Waith, bounded by three concentric walls. It covered a chamber, now roofless, measuring 21 feet in length and agreeing in general plan with the stalled cairn of Yarso on Rousay (p. 16). But it is divided into five compartments; from the central one a small beehive cell opens in the rear wall.

When originally excavated in 1884, fragments of over 22 pottery bowls, several flint implements and arrow-heads—all calcined—and many human remains were recovered. The ornate vases (now in the National Museum at Edinburgh) have given the name of the cairn to a class of decorated neolithic pottery now familiar also from Rousay and Eday, but peculiar to the Orkneys and perhaps North Uist.

The Dwarfie Stane on Hoy is a huge block of sandstone in which a chamber has been quarried. It was designed, as C. S. T. Calder was the first to recognize in 1937, as a burial vault with the same plan and of the same general age as the other Orcadian tombs already described, but cut in the rock. Rock-cut chamber tombs are very common in the Mediterranean and recur in Portugal and other parts of the Atlantic megalithic province. There they are contemporary with the more familiar built tombs. In Great Britain, however, the Dwarfie Stane is unique, though a couple of possible rock-cut tombs have now been recognized in Ireland.

Another class of chamber tombs, peculiar to Orkney but having analogues in Ireland and abroad, is constructed on a different principle to the foregoing: a variable number of small beehive cells, presumably designed as the actual burial-places, open off a lofty central chamber, itself entered by a passage. No distinctive relics certainly accompanying the primary interments have been recovered from any of these tombs and it is quite likely that all were built at a later period than any of the tombs hitherto considered—to a period in fact when copper and/or bronze was already used all over Scotland. Yet it is convenient to describe the group here, for it comprises four monuments under the Ministry's care.

Maes Howe covers the finest "megalithic tomb" in the British Isles, the masonry of which is surpassed nowhere in Western Europe. The tumulus rises from a flat plain at the south-east end of the Loch of Harray, and belongs to a great complex of monuments to which we shall return. The imposing mound is 115 feet in diameter and still 24 feet high. It is encircled, 50 feet to 70 feet from its base, by a great penannular ditch, 45 feet wide. From the south-east edge of the barrow a passage now over 36 feet long leads to a chamber 15 feet square and now 12 feet 6 inches high. (The original corbelled roof is preserved to that height only, the gap being covered by modern vaulting). In the middle of each side wall save the southern a rectangular "window" some 3 feet above the floor gives access to a small rectangular cell, 3 feet 6 inches high, and roofed by a single lintel slab. These cells, the actual depositories of the deceased, could be plugged with stone blocks, still lying near them on the chamber floor.

The masonry of the passage and chamber is of outstanding excellence. Most of the stones used have been dressed. The walls and roof of the inner part of the passage are formed of monoliths, on an average 18 feet 6 inches long, 4 feet 4 inches wide and 7 inches thick. The joints are so finely adjusted that it is impossible to insert a knife-blade between them. Projecting piers in the chamber's four corners, ingeniously designed to support the corbels, are each faced on one side with upright monoliths that attain a height of 9 feet 8 inches.

Maes Howe was presumably designed as the burial place of a potent chief and recalls in several details some famous tombs on the Boyne. It was opened by Farrer in 1861, who found he had been anticipated by Vikings in the 12th century. These had left nothing of the original burials nor their furniture, but a record of their violation in the form of Runic inscriptions and engravings of a lion, a walrus, and a serpent-knot. The inscriptions mention the removal of treasures and record various visits by Christian Vikings and crusaders about A.D. 1150.

In scale and magnificence Maes Howe is unique in Great Britain. But the idea of its internal arrangement is reproduced in rougher masonry, but combined with familiar Orcadian features, in other chambered tumuli. Three such are to be found just across the ridge separating the plain from the foreshores of the Bay of Firth. Two stand on hillsides overlooking the Bay, the third, Quanterness, at the foot of the second hill.

Cuween Hill. A mound just below the crest of this hill covers an irregular chamber some 11 feet long and 7 feet 6 inches high, but under 6 feet wide. It is entered by a very low passage that debouches at the south end of the east side. North of its mouth in the same wall is the entrance to a cell and three other cells open respectively off the opposite side and the two end walls. Bones of men, dogs and oxen were discovered, when the chamber was opened in 1901.

Wideford Hill. On the west slope of this hill and across a valley opposite the last-named tomb, some 350 feet above the sea, stands a conspicuous tumulus defined by three concentric walls. It covers a chamber, built as at Cuween Hill, in an excavation in the hillside. The chamber, entered from the east by a passage, is 10 feet long, 4 feet 6 inches wide and 8 feet high. Three large cells open off it, one measuring

6 feet 6 inches by 4 feet 6 inches by 7 feet. The chamber was first explored by Petrie in 1849 who found only animal bones in it.

At the foot of the same hill ¾ of a mile to the north-east rises the barrow of Quanterness, nearly 130 feet in diameter and still 14 feet high. It is known to cover a chamber similar in plan to that at

Quoyness, on the eastern shore of the Elsness peninsula on the island of Sanday. The mound, girt by a triple retaining wall, now rises over 12 feet high from a raised platform and is 60 feet in diameter. The main chamber, now roofless, is roughly rectangular, 12 feet 6 inches north-south and 5 feet 6 inches east-west; its converging walls stand over 12 feet high. Two beehive cells open from each side and one from each end. The entrance passage debouches midway between the two cells on the south side. Human skeletons were found in the cells, on the chamber floor and even in the passage. Implements, two stone and one bone, and pot sherds recovered bear a resemblance to some found, at Skara Brae (p. 21).

On the *Holm of Papa Westray* rises a chambered tumulus, allied in conception to the foregoing, but of quite extravagant proportions. The chamber is no less than 67 feet long but only 5 feet wide and was once at least 9 feet high. It is divided into three subdivisions by transverse walls that do not run quite across it. Fourteen beehive cells open off the chamber which is entered by a short passage through the south-east side. On the lintel of the east cell and on a slab in the west wall of the southern-most subdivision are some curious engravings. One recalls the "eyes-and-eyebrows" motive encountered in megalithic tombs or on the pottery therefrom both in Denmark and in Atlantic Europe. Engravings—or paintings—are not unfamiliar on the walls of megalithic tombs in the Iberian Peninsula, the Paris basin, Brittany and Ireland. The signs just described from Papa Westray and a spiral design from a ruined cairn on Eday are the sole examples of this megalithic art in Scotland.

"Steinacleit" Cairn and Stone Circle. The remnants of a chambered cairn with stone circle kerb are preserved at Steinacleit half a mile S.S.E. of Lower Shader Schoolhouse, in Lewis. Amid the loose stones of the cairn three uprights probably mark the chamber. The kerb which is about 50 feet in diameter consists of ten uprights. Peat digging revealed a ring of stones forming an oval enclosure in the south-west portion of which the cairn is situated. The enclosure lies east to west and measures 270 feet by 183 feet. No attempt seems to have been made to form a wall of the ring which is composed of fairly close-set stones, single in height and varying from 5 to 6 feet broad down to a single stone's width.

The stupendous funerary monuments just surveyed conjure up pictures of neolithic voyages on the Atlantic that would be incredible to those unacquainted with the more recent navigation of the Polynesians, when they were no better equipped. But the dwellings of the megalith-builders were less substantial than their tombs, and none is known in Great Britain. But there were other groups inhabiting Britain in neolithic times—or rather in a neolithic stage of culture. One such group was living in eastern England and the Lothians at, or just before, the beginning of the local Bronze Age, but there they are known only by their pottery that is quite distinct from that usually found in megalithic tombs. Some of these people had reached Orkney before the Beaker-folk initiated a Bronze Age in the islands and built there houses that give an unique and astonishing picture of life in the neolithic stage. For in default of timber on the treeless islands they had not only to build their huts of stone, but also to translate into stone articles of furniture that would normally be made of perishable wood; for that purpose as remarked on p. 11 the local Caithness flag stone was particularly well adapted.

Skara Brae reveals a cluster of such neolithic dwellings preserved in drift sand. There were at least eight, but several have been partially demolished by the sea, for the site lies on the shore of the Bay of Skaill exposed to the violence of the open Atlantic. Luckily some of the houses were completely buried in, and choked with, sand, so that their walls still stand intact in places to a height of over 8 feet. The roofs, however, are gone beyond reconstruction.

A typical dwelling is a rectangular room with rounded corners some 15 feet to 20 feet square. It was entered through a low, narrow doorway, less than 5 feet high, that could be closed by a stone slab fastened by a bar that slid in bar-holes cut in the stone door jambs. A peat fire burned on a square, kerbed hearth in the middle of the room. On either side enclosures framed by slabs on edge served as beds—naturally lined with heather or hay. Each bed could be covered by a canopy of skins supported by stone bedposts which still survive. Recesses in the wall above it would serve as keeping places for the personal possessions of the bed's occupants. A two-shelved stone dresser was built against the rear wall. Tanks, framed with slate slabs and luted to hold liquids, were let into the floor. Cells in the thickness of the walls may have served as store cupboards or perhaps as privies. Some are served by drains such as run under the floor of every house.

The better to exclude draughts due to the continuous gales, "midden"—ash, dung and rubbish mixed with sand—was piled round the house-walls and kept in place by retaining walls. Eventually all the spaces between the huts were packed with midden, and the alleys joining them were walled and roofed with stone and then also buried in midden. A well-built sewer, which can now be visited by trapdoors, drained the complex. The whole must have looked like a great anthill with crater-like smoke-holes over each dwelling and two or three tunnel-like entries on the flanks. The eastern exit of the main alley has been washed away, but on the west it opened through a door on to a paved area. Beyond this is a single free-standing building (No. 8 on the plan). This contains no beds and a kiln instead of a dresser. The settlement thus represents a remarkably efficient adjustment to an intemperate clime.

Its inhabitants lived by breeding cows and sheep and collecting shellfish. There is no evidence that they hunted or fished, nor that they cultivated barley as the megalith-builders had done. Nor is a textile industry attested; the villagers presumably dressed in skins which they certainly fastened with bone pins. They displayed great dexterity in fashioning implements, vessels and ornaments out of local materials, but used no imported substances.

Evidence from a similar village at Rinyo on Rousay implies that Skara Brae was still inhabited when the Beaker folk began to land in Orkney. But the artificially buried village just described is the last of several similar settlements, built one over the other, on the same site. The foundations of three houses, identical in plan with the later ones, can still be seen under the latter's walls, and under these test pits revealed a still earlier occupation by the same people. Parallel observations were made at Rinyo in 1946, but there some pottery from the deeper, and therefore older, levels resembles the Onston ware found in local megalithic tombs. Hence Rinyo and Skara Brae go back to the time when chambered tombs were still being used for burial in Orkney. They are thus neolithic in a second sense. That, of course, need not mean that they are fabulously old. The first houses at Skara Brae may, indeed, have been erected as late as 1200 B.C.—a time when bronze had long been current in southern England and when iron was replacing it for tools in Hither Asia. Even so it is surprising to find that people in such a stage of culture lived in such commodious, well-drained and nicely furnished houses. Further south people in the same stage must have been just as well off at an earlier date, but all the evidence has perished and, but for Skara Brae, would have been unsuspected.

THE BRONZE AGE

The use of metal tools and weapons—copper and bronze preceded iron by about 2,000 years—presupposes not only a knowledge of metallurgy—of the mysteries of mining, smelting and casting—but also organized trade to distribute the products; for copper lodes are infrequent and there is no tin at all in Scotland. In fact metal was at first very rare and costly, and metal objects are quite exceptional in the graves assigned to the Bronze Age in Scotland. But indications of trade in other materials—flint, lignite, amber—are prominent from the first.

The new archæological stage was ushered in reputedly by the advent of the Beaker-folk. These are supposed to be invaders, since their skeletons are normally round-headed, while those found in megalithic tombs and at Skara Brae are all long-headed. They were buried individually, normally in short cists or coffins designed to contain a single crouched skeleton, and the Beaker from which they get their name seems to mark a complete break with neolithic traditions in potting. On the other hand the Beaker-folk were not so much the bringers as the first purchasers of metal tools, weapons and ornaments. Such were at first obtained from Ireland. During what may be called the Early Bronze Age, while Beakers were everywhere the only fashionable thing to bury with the dead, metal was used mainly for weapons and ornaments. Subsequently in the Middle Bronze Age which certainly began about 1500 B.C. in southern England and not very much later on the Scottish mainland, fashions changed, save in Aberdeenshire; very ornate vases, termed Food Vessels, were deposited in graves. At the same time metal became more common. Merchant artificers and prospectors travelled about Scotland, and probably began exploiting surface lodes of copper ore. The itinerant traders followed regular routes, now known to us from articles which they lost. This trade was already international; Irish, and perhaps also Scottish, manufactures found their way to Scandinavia and North Germany. Irish metalwork was brought by sea to landfalls on the Clyde and the Firth of Lorne, and thence transported overland to be reshipped from the Tay estuary and the mouth of the Dee.

Finally a new cultural group spread over Scotland; they have been named the Urn-folk, because they cremated their dead and buried the ashes under large Cinerary Urns mostly of the Overhanging Rim family. (Of course cremation had been practised occasionally even while Beakers were fashionable, and Food Vessels contain calcined bones rather more often). Some of the Urn-folk had slowly spread north from southern England, bringing the tradition of the Overhanging Rim urn with them, but in Scotland they are mixed with elements of the older population, whose ashes were contained in urns that embody native traditions.

The Late Bronze Age is further characterized by a relative abundance of metal due to improvements in extractive and processing techniques and a reorganization of the distributive side of the industry. As a consequence bronze was used for tools to be employed in rough work and agriculture, as well as by craftsmen, and for large objects, such as cauldrons and shields. Indeed, bronze was probably so cheap in Scotland and Ireland that it could successfully compete with iron for several centuries.

Throughout the Bronze Age most people still lived by subsistence farming. While flax as well as cereals were demonstrably grown, the cultivation must have been of the "shifting" kind under which a small plot is tilled—with hoes—until exhausted and then abandoned for a fresh patch of virgin soil. But animal husbandry, always combined with hunting, seems now to have become relatively more important than agriculture. As a consequence perhaps dwellings were more temporary and unsubstantial than in the preceding "Age". In fact throughout the British Isles with the solitary exceptions of Shetland and Scilly no Bronze Age houses are known at all, but only small circular foundations, suitable for some kind of tent-like superstructure. Such are common on Scottish moors, but only a few of them, notably a couple near Muirkirk, in Ayrshire, are at all likely to belong to the Bronze Age.

Even more than in the Neolithic Age men devoted more care to durable dwellings for the dead than to houses for the living, and appear to have spent more energy and labour on the preparation for rites than on what we regard as practical ends. This is just what is observed today among illiterate tribes in Australia, New Guinea or Africa. In any case the extant monuments of the Bronze Age are of a ritual character. They are often impressive for all that, and constitute romantic and imposing additions to the natural landscape. They may conveniently be divided into three classes: sepulchres; standing stones, either isolated or forming circles and alignments, the precise function of which is unknown, and finally geometrical carvings either on the living rock or on stones connected with the preceding classes.

BURIAL CAIRNS. Bronze Age people or at least those of a certain rank were buried under cairns or earthen tumuli. In contrast to some neolithic cairns, those of the Bronze Age are always round. But these, too, were seldom, if ever, mere random piles of stone or earth. Some are of great size, and when they stand, as many do, on the tops of hills, are very conspicuous. They normally cover one or more cists of slabs, containing a crouched skeleton or perhaps cremated bones. The majority of such cairns were built in the Early or Middle Bronze Age. Most cremated burials of the Late Bronze Age were contained in urns placed inverted in the bare earth without a covering mound or inserted into earlier barrows. But even in the Late Bronze Age cairns were still erected over the graves of important personages.

It has seldom been necessary for the Ministry to intervene actively to conserve Bronze Age cairns. A fine example preserved from destruction is the cairn of *Memsie* near Fraserburgh, the last remaining of a group of three; the others were partially demolished in the last quarter of the eighteenth century when human bones were found in them and finally removed some eighty years later. The cairn is circular with an approximate diameter of 80 feet and still stands to a height of 30 feet. While a very large number have been protected by scheduling, only a tiny fraction are actually under guardianship. Still, a very representative series is grouped on the Poltalloch estate near Kilmartin.

Mid Cairn, Nether Largie, is one of the line of great cairns in the Kilmartin valley, mentioned on p. 10. It stands some 400 yards north of the cairn originally erected to cover the Neolithic segmented cist then described. The Mid Cairn was about 110 feet in diameter, but had been grievously despoiled before it was placed under the Ministry's guardianship. In 1929 J. H. Craw found that it covered two burial cists, but both had already been emptied of their contents. The northernmost of the two, framed by four schist slabs, is 4 feet long, 2 feet 4 inches wide, and 2 feet deep. It was carefully paved with water-worn pebbles and covered by an unnecessarily big cap-stone over 8 feet long by 6 feet wide. In the side slabs grooves have been hammered out into which the end slabs fit—a practice very common between Kilmartin and Crinan, but otherwise only noted in the Scilly Isles. The other cist is smaller, but there is a cup-mark on the north end slab. Five cup marks adorn the lower face of a slab which lay on the ground just within the kerb bounding the cairn.

The North Cairn, Nether Largie, 150 yards from the foregoing was about 70 feet in diameter and stood nearly 9 feet high when excavated in 1930. Mr. Craw removed 300 cartloads of water-worn boulders which were built into a wall round the central area. This was defined by a low bank some 45 feet in diameter. At the centre is a cist, 5 feet 2 inches long, 2 feet 4 inches wide and 1 foot 10 inches deep, and framed as usual by four slabs. The cap-stone measured 6 feet 7 inches by 3 feet 5 inches by 9 inches, and was itself covered by 18 large flat slabs. On its underside are carved 41 cup marks and 10 shallow representations of flat copper axe-heads. Two larger representations of axe-heads adorn the inner face of the north end slab. This cist had once contained an unburnt human body of which only the crown of a tooth survived. To the north was an oval pit, 5 feet long, 2 feet 6 inches wide and 2 feet 9 inches deep. South of the central cist a large flat slab was found lying on the ground. Near it a small erect slab is decorated with two irregular circles.

Cup-marks, i.e. circular depressions hammered out of the rock with a sort of chisel-like punch of flint or copper, are quite often associated with burial monuments of the Middle Bronze Age. Representations of real objects, in contrast to geometrical symbols, are very exceptional in the Bronze Age art of the British Isles. Abroad a variety of scenes, e.g. in Scandinavia, were then depicted on tomb walls or on the living rock, and in Brittany hafted axes are among the varied symbols carved in megalithic tombs. But the closest analogies to our axe-heads are to be found on a stone from a barrow in Dorset and again in the Kilmartin district, less than a mile south of Nether Largie.

At *Ri Cruin* a large cairn on the crest of a low, gravelly ridge once covered three cists. Some time before 1870 a lime-kiln was built on the west flank of the ridge and the cairn despoiled for stones, when the cists were exposed. The southernmost and largest is 6 feet 5 inches long, 3 feet wide, and 2 feet 9 inches deep and is framed by seven slabs. The single slab forming the west end bears eight shallow representations of axe-heads similar to those at Nether Largie. A narrow slab in the east end was ornamented with a figure like a rake. This slab has been replaced by another of similar size and is known only from a cast. the rake-like figure has been interpreted as a representation of a boat, but this interpretation has been disputed.

The axe figures, being shallow impressions or negatives, were once thought to be moulds in which actual metal axes were cast. Stone moulds for flat axes are well known, but the depressions are very much deeper than any on the Kilmartin cist slabs. The latter are purely symbolic. They emphasize the magic potency attributed to the new metal tool and weapon in the Early Bronze Age. They may indicate, too, that trade in copper or its extraction made a substantial contribution to the prosperity of the communities living in the Kilmartin valley and to the wealth of their chiefs. Reference has already been made to the copper lodes in the district and to the trade routes that traverse it. Now it has been noted elsewhere in Britain and on the Continent —Denmark offers the most striking illustration—that Bronze Age barrows lie along ancient trackways. So in the Kilmartin valley the cairns already mentioned, together with others and various Standing Stones (including a striking group just south of Nether Largie), mark the old route that continued on across the Add to reach the waters of Loch Fyne at Lochgilphead. The same complex comprises two other sepulchral monuments under the Ministry's guardianship.

Dunchraigaig is the site of a great cairn, once over 100 feet in diameter, that was "excavated" in 1864 by Canon Greenwell and earlier by Dean Mapleton. Greenwell exposed two cists. One in the south quadrant of the denuded cairn can be entered through one of its sides, for it is framed not with the usual slabs, but with rudely-built walls of boulders. This cist is nearly 10 feet long and is 5 feet wide at its east end. The coverstone is a gigantic block, 13 feet by 6 feet by 1 foot 3 inches that must weigh over 5 tons! Remains of several burnt bodies and unburnt skeletons are said to have been found in this chamber, that in size, too, recalls a Neolithic family vault more than a Bronze Age cist.

Higher up in the body of the cairn towards the north is a normal short cist. This contained a particularly handsome bowl of the Food Vessel type and cremated bones. But an unburnt skeleton was found under the cist's floor and another lying crouched on the capstone. Greenwell found a third cist containing a Food Vessel and cremated remains which are no longer visible.

This cairn lies on a terrace on the east side of Kilmartin Burn, half a mile south-east of the cists at Ri Cruin. North-west of the latter lies

The Temple Wood Stone Circle. This originally consisted of a ring of 20 slabs set on end with their faces on the circumference of a circle, 43 feet to 40 feet 6 inches in diameter. Several stones have been broken and six are amissing, though their sockets or stumps were identified by Craw in 1929. Near the centre is a cist measuring 5 feet by 2 feet 11 in. by 1 foot 9 inches. The monument is accordingly funerary, erected to mark and guard symbolically an important burial.

BRONZE AGE ART

In addition to the exceptional representations on the slabs of cists, geometrical patterns inscribed on smooth surfaces of living rock are very numerous between Kilmartin and Crinan. The standard pattern is a cup-like depression surrounded by one to seven concentric circles. Sometimes a single gutter runs from the central cup across the encircling rings. In all cases the designs have been executed by the same hammering or "pecking" process illustrated by the sepulchral monuments. They are usually found on sloping rock surfaces, smoothed by ice or other natural agency. Since their execution most have become covered with turf or peat which has preserved them, and they have only been exposed by the accidents of turf-cutting or by shrinkage of the peat. Some of the most typical groups are kept clear by the Ministry and surrounded by a fence to prevent damage by cattle.

At *Baluachraig*, a little south of Dunchraigaig Cairn, are several groups on rocks in the terrace east of Kilmartin Burn, below the main road from Kilmartin to Lochgilphead. Another group lies on the west side of the Burn at

Ballygowan. A third protected group will be found further south in the Add Valley west of the school at

Kilmichael Glassary. Still further south and nearer the bay of Loch Fyne termed Loch Gilp are two more groups.

Achnabreck is about a quarter of a mile east of the Kilmartin-Lochgilphead road, opposite the junction with the Crinan road. Close to the farm the exposed crest of a rocky ridge is covered with well-preserved scribings.

Near Cairnbaan Hotel, on the banks of the Crinan canal, is another group that has been celebrated since 1860.

Cup-and-ring marked rocks are fairly widely distributed in the British Isles. They are particularly dense in the West Riding of Yorkshire, in Northumberland round Rothbury, and in Galloway. There the Ministry has charge of two groups near Port William at *Big Balcraig* and *Drumtroddan*.

Simple cup-marks have an immense distribution and were already being carved by Neanderthal "men" in the Old Stone Age, perhaps 100,000 years ago, but cup-and-ring marks of the type just described are practically confined to the British Isles and to the metalliferous district of north-west Spain and north Portugal. The restriction of this art to two tin-producing countries (after Cornwall, Galicia has the richest deposits in Western Europe) in an age when tin was specially important to men, may indicate connections by sea between the north-western corner of the Iberian Peninsula and the British Isles. Here these markings occur, apart from rock-surfaces, on stones in the Avenue leading to Avebury in Wiltshire, and in cists, several of which contained Food Vessels. Hence the cup-and-ring style was established here by the beginning of the Middle Bronze Age and is connected in some sense with the Food Vessel Culture. In any case it is contrasted with all groups of representational art on the one hand and with the geometric art of megalithic tombs on the other.

One school of interpreters believes that the pattern is but an extremely conventionalized version of the human figure. But though cup-and-

Plate 7. *Stalled cairn, Midhowe, Orkney*

Plate 8. *Excavated burial in reconstructed cairn, Cairnpapple, West Lothian*

Plate 8. *Excavated burial in reconstructed cairn, Cairnpapple, West Lothian*

Plate 7. *Stalled cairn, Midhowe, Orkney*

Plate 9. *Broch of Gurness, Aikerness, Orkney*

Plate 10. *Maiden Stone, Aberdeenshire*

ring marks are doubtless symbols, their symbolism is surely more esoteric than that. Aborigines in Central Australia still trace similar patterns in the sand and read them as records, or rather illustrations, of mythical events. The Australian patterns have indeed been described as "primitive maps", but the territory mapped seems to be usually ritual. Despite a plausible connection with the metal industry, it would be rash to regard the scribings round Kilmartin or round Ilkley as maps of routes that probably did pass in their immediate vicinity.

SEPULCHRAL CIRCLES. The graves of persons of peculiar eminence or sanctity were sometimes surrounded with a ring of upright stones. A simple example in the Kilmartin district has already been described. Others are more grandiose.

A very specialized variety, confined to the coasts of the Beauly Firth and the valleys of the Nairn and Spey, is best represented by the group at Clava under the Ministry's guardianship. Monuments of this class are generally marked "Stone Circles" on the Ordnance Survey Maps, and some in fact appear today as three concentric rings of great stones. In reality even these are just the most stubborn remnants of chambered cairns of what Childe once termed the Beauly class. The innermost ring constituted the foundation for a chamber's wall; the next bounded and supported the cairn that covered it. Only the outer ring originally consisted of free standing uprights. In the cases mentioned the smaller boulders forming the cairn have been carted away.

The inner and middle rings in fact consist of massive rounded boulders set close together. The outermost alone comprises tall monoliths. Stones in one or more rings are quite often adorned with cup marks.

No cairn of the Clava (or Beauly) class has yielded any relics to provide archæologists with a clue as to the relative age of its erection. They are classed as "Bronze Age" here in view of their relation on the one hand to the Boyne tombs of Eire, on the other to the Recumbent Stone circles of Aberdeenshire. But of course the same term could be applied just as well to Maes Howe and kindred Orcadian tombs. Nevertheless, apart from a group in Strathspey, near Aviemore, Clava cairns do seem to lie along a Bronze Age trade-route well defined by the distribution of characteristic weapons. The Recumbent Stone circles exhibit a complementary distribution along the eastern continuation of the same route.

The Cairns of Clava stand on the flood plain of the Nairn in the narrow gorge immediately below the battlefield of Culloden Moor. They were opened in 1828, when sherds of a rough clay urn, now lost, were recovered from one.

Cairn I, the most westerly, is surrounded by a circle of 11 upright monoliths; four of the stones had fallen and were replaced last century, perhaps rather out of position; there was probably once a 12th stone. The cairn, with an overall diameter of 53 feet, is surrounded by a kerb of large boulders, interrupted by a gap opposite the tallest uprights. This is the entrance to a passage, bordered by similar boulders, 2 feet wide and once 4½ feet high. It leads to a chamber some 12½ feet in diameter. The ring of large boulders on edge that frames it supports courses of rubble masonry oversailing one another inwards. This masonry must originally have been carried up to form a corbelled dome over the whole space, about 12 feet above the floor. A cup-mark is observable on one stone in the chamber wall.

Cairn II, on the east, agrees with No. I in its general lay-out. The passage-wall includes a cup-marked stone.

Cairn III, in the middle, differs from the foregoing in that no passage gives access to the interior; the kerb and the chamber wall are both unbroken rings. There is no trace of masonry above the uprights surrounding the chamber which is 22 feet across and may never have been roofed. A peculiarity of Cairn III is constituted by three stone "causeways" radiating from the base of the kerb out to uprights in the outer ring on the south, east and north-west.

Several other cairns of the Beauly class, too, demonstrably covered similar closed "chambers". Such, then, cannot be regarded as "family vaults"; they were rather erected to house once and for all the mortal remains of a single chief.

The Clava cemetery comprises other smaller cairns that have never been examined, and that in 1945 were scarcely distinguishable for scrub and brambles. Moreover, it may join on to another cemetery upstream, which, lying on long cultivated land, is in a still more ruinous condition.

Recumbent Stone Circles. A group of over 70 monuments in Banffshire, Aberdeenshire and Kincardineshire has a distribution complementary to that of Clava cairns. The distinctive feature which gives its name to the group is a huge monolith, lying on its side between the two tallest uprights—termed Flankers—of an exceedingly irregular circle. The Recumbent may be 16 feet long and 8 feet high but its upper side is generally straight and usually laid so as to be strictly horizontal. It would, therefore, provide a good "artificial horizon" for observing astronomical phenomena, such as the heliacal rising or setting of a star, that were used by the priestly astronomers of Oriental antiquity for correcting the calendar.

Only two such circles have been scientifically examined. All have been disturbed by less skilful excavations, by treasure-seekers, by tree-planting, stone quarrying, agricultural operations and sometimes at least by prehistoric communities before the beginning of our era. Nevertheless it seems likely that the ring of uprights and Recumbent surrounded a ring cairn. There is some evidence that the central space enclosed by the cairn contained the cremated remains of a great chief or magician. Scraps of pottery from the two excavated circles alone support the belief that this original occupant of the monument belonged to the Beaker-folk. (It must be recalled that Beakers remained fashionable in this area much longer than anywhere else in Britain). Plentiful relics, however, prove that these sacred sites were used for some purpose by people of quite different traditions who occupied north-east Scotland shortly before the commencement of the Christian era. These played such havoc with the supposed earlier interments that the ambiguous evidence from only two sites does not suffice to establish conclusively the erection and use of these circles while Beakers were still fasionable locally. It will be best to summarize what Kilbride-Jones actually found, when he supervised the Ministry's conservation work at one typical circle.

The Loanhead Stone Circle, in Daviot, stands just below the summit of a small rounded hill, some 500 feet above the sea, commanding a wide view in all directions save to the north-west. The circle consists of 10 monoliths, 5 of which were prostrate in 1934, and measures only 64 feet across. The Recumbent Stone on the south-south-west is just over 11 feet long and 7 feet wide, but had split longitudinally so as to look like two stones. The subsoil had been scooped out to accommodate its underside. The two flankers have been truncated, but that on the west still stands 7 feet 2 inches high. The eastern one has been re-erected; it is embedded only 5 inches in the soil. The third upright west of the Recumbent is the tallest, being 8 feet 3 inches long, but 1 foot 5 inches of this length is underground. Its socket is cut down through the subsoil to the rock and wedging stones had been inserted to help in balancing the mass. All the uprights had rather pointed bases and were slid into their sockets from the same side. (Their erectors, of course, had no windlass nor crane to help in manoeuvring the heavy blocks). All have been trimmed by removing projecting irregularities, but none is dressed. Five cup-marks in a vertical line adorn the north face of stone 9 (reading clockwise from the west flanker).

A very irregular and incomplete kerb defines the enclosed ring cairn that just abuts on the circle at the base of the east flanker. This cairn may have measured 54 feet across, but has been much disturbed and despoiled. Within the former area of the cairn and presumably buried by it, a crescentic setting of upright stones has been exposed in the south-east quadrant and roughly concentric with the kerb. It apparently marked one side of the pyre, on which a body had been cremated before the cairn was heaped; for west of the setting the cairn stones covered a layer of dark soil, containing fragments of calcined bone and charcoal.

At the centre of the cairn was a shallow pit that may well have been designed to contain the ashes of the personage cremated on the pyre immediately to the east. A few sherds of Beaker were found in this pit; they constitute the most solid evidence for the belief that the monument was originally erected in the Beaker period. But the pit had certainly been used both for culinary and funerary purposes at the end of the Bronze Age. Most of the pottery found in it was of the kind characteristic of the transition from the Bronze to the Iron Age, and the cremated bones from the pit seem to have belonged to the same period.

Other parts of the monument had been disturbed at the same time. Small cairns have been heaped at the bases of most uprights. In that in front of stone 4 was found a Transitional pot, containing cremated human bones, and similar pottery was found in other small cairns and widely distributed over the whole area of the circle. Transitional pottery, stone ladles or other relics appropriate to the same epoch have been found in other Recumbent Stone Circles, and led to the belief that all had been erected at the end of the Bronze Age. But the same pottery was recovered from one fossed circle in the county, a type of monument elsewhere dated to the Early Bronze Age. The numerous Beaker sherds discovered by Kilbride-Jones at Loanhead and a single sherd from Old Keig suggest rather that Recumbent Stone Circles were erected in the Beaker period. In the Transitional period they—and at least one fossed circle—were disturbed and re-used, perhaps for profane purposes. Further observations at Loanhead strengthen this view.

A small cairn abutting against the base of stone 8 on the east but outside the circle covers a small cist which contained calcined bones and a dominutive Food Vessel, assignable to the beginning of the Late Bronze Age when Urn-folk (p. 23) had already reached Aberdeenshire.

Just south of this cist, but still within the Ministry's boundary fence, is a roughly circular area, some 36 feet across, bounded by a shallow trench. This probably formed the foundation for a dyke, and is interrupted on the north-east and south-west and on the north, where the cist lies on the line of the trench. It enclosed a Late Bronze Age cemetery in which one body had been cremated *in situ*, so that the calcined bones lay on the floor of the pyre, while the ashes of thirty other individuals were deposited in normal Cinerary Urns or in the bare earth. One cremation was enclosed in a Transitional vessel, and Transitional pottery was found in the earth over the urns. Similar round cemeteries or urnfields have been reported elsewhere in Britain, but this is the only example preserved.

East Aquhorthies Stone Circle. This is one of the best preserved examples of the recumbent stone circle class. Situated in the district of Garioch, Aberdeenshire. It consists of a ring of 12 upright porphyrite stones several of which are over four feet in width and range in height from 3 feet 10 inches to 5 feet 10 inches. The large recumbent stone of reddish granite over 12 feet in length is flanked by two uprights on the south arc. The interior of the circle, grassy and rendered slightly uneven by small stones, rises gently towards the centre.

Tomnaverie Stone Circle. The remains of a stone circle preserved under guardianship in the parish of Coull, Aberdeenshire. Only five stones remain erect, set almost precisely in the circumference of a true circle, 56 feet in diameter. A recumbent stone, 11 feet 3 inches long and 5 feet broad, is set on the same circumference and flanked by earthfast stones. There are indications of two concentric settings within the outer circle but their nature is confused pending systematic excavation.

Torhouse Stone Circle, Wigtownshire. A circle of nineteen boulders, apparently complete, stands on the edge of a low mound about 20 yards in diameter. In the centre of the circle are three boulders set in a line, a comparatively small one between two larger stones. The tallest stone of the circle is 4 feet 9 inches high, and the largest stones seem all to lie along the south-eastern arc of the circle. Many small stones just under or above the grass within the circle may indicate that in origin it is a sepulchral monument.

The Standing Stones of Cullerlie, Echt, illustrate a different type of sepulchral circle. They stand on a bed of gravel in a generally low-lying and swampy plain. The circle consists of eight stones and is 32 feet in diameter. The components are untrimmed, natural boulders, and the tallest, on the north, stands only 6 feet high. The area they enclose had been consecrated by fires which had baked the subsoil and reddened the uprights. After this preparation eight small cairns had been piled on the consecrated ground. Each is defined by a ring of boulders, that round the central cairn being double. All but one had been disturbed before the Ministry took charge of the monument. At the centre of the intact cairn was a pit, 21 inches deep and 28 inches across, which contained charcoal and cremated bone. A pyre had apparently been kindled in or over this pit. Similar observations were made in the other cairns, but no relics were discovered to indicate the age of the cremations.

Small circles of comparable dimensions are not uncommon on Scottish moors, but have yielded no satisfactory evidence of date. All probably belong to the Bronze Age, but perhaps fall nearer its end than its beginning.

NON-SEPULCHRAL CIRCLES. That some monuments defined by rings of standing stones were not constructed primarily to contain burials has been demonstrated by excavations at the world-famous Circles of Stonehenge and Avebury and less celebrated constructions on the same plan. The essential feature of the relevant monuments is that a ring of upright monoliths is itself enclosed by a wide ditch or fosse, interrupted by one or more causeways and generally surrounded in turn by a bank. The same excavations have produced evidence that the monuments existed while Beakers were in fashion locally but may have been erected before the arrival of Beaker-folk. They naturally provided no indication as to the beliefs inspiring the stupendous labour involved in transporting and erecting the gigantic monoliths and excavating with antler picks, bone shovels and naked hands the encircling fosse. Nor can the solemn and magically potent ceremonies performed in them be reconstructed. In Scotland, fossed circles have been identified in the Lothians (Cairnpapple Hill near Linlithgow), in Aberdeenshire near Inverurie, and in Orkney. Three of the finest are under the Ministry's guardianship.

Cairnpapple is situated on a hilltop between Linlithgow and Bathgate, overlooking the Firth of Forth six miles to the north. It had a long history extending from late Neolithic times, about 2000 B.C. to the first century A.D. The site was first chosen for a sanctuary and cemetery. With stone axes manufactured in North Wales and the Lake District, an area of oak and hazel scrub was cleared on the summit of the hill and an irregular arc of seven holes dug, open to the west, to contain a series of standing stones. In and near these a dozen deposits of cremated human bones were made. A century or two later about 1800 B.C., the site was remodelled as a monumental open-air temple on a large scale. Twenty-six large stones were set up in an oval within an area 145 feet by 125 feet defined by a rock-cut ditch 12 feet in width with an external bank and entrance causeways to north and south about 30 feet across. Within the area a ceremonial burial was made at the foot of a standing stone within a stone kerb and small cairn. Another burial was made beside one of the stones of the main oval setting on the east.

By 1500 B.C. the sanctity of the site appears to have been forgotten. The old shrine was despoiled to make a burial cairn for a Bronze Age chief. The stones were taken down to form the great kerb of the circular cairn and its massive cists, one containing an inhumation with a Food Vessel pot, the other a cremation.

Later in the Bronze Age, about 1000 B.C., burials were added to the tomb by enlarging the cairn to twice its size thus concealing many of the older features. In this enlargement, which had its own stone kerb, were two burials by cremation beneath inverted Bronze Age urns.

In the Iron Age, possibly in the first century or so A.D., four burials at full length were made within the ditched area.

The Ring of Brogar, on the isthmus between the Lochs of Harray and Stenness is one of the great complex of monuments of which Maes Howe is also a member. The ring stands not quite on the crest of the ridge separating the two lochs. It now consists of 27 upright slabs, set with their broad faces tangential to a circle 340 feet in diameter. Some stones are clearly missing. Many of the survivors are mere stumps and others are badly weathered. The tallest now stands 15 feet above the ground, and none is likely to have been less than 8 feet high. It is thought that the slabs have been brought from an ancient quarry on Vestra Fiold, some 6 miles away. On one upright on the north is cut an undeciphered runic inscription and a cross.

The stones stand on a gently sloping space, 10 feet to 12 feet from the inner lip of the enclosing fosse. This seems on an average 30 feet wide, but has never been excavated. It is spanned by causeways on the north-west and south-east, but no trace of bank is visible outside it.

The adjacent fields have yielded quite a harvest of flint arrowheads and broken stone mace-heads of Bronze Age type. To the north, just across the boundary of Sandwick Parish, is a ruined chamber tomb and close by, the Ring of Bookan, an irregular area surrounded by a fosse. Nearer to Brogar are several large earthen barrows, most probably heaped in the Bronze Age. There is a similar concentration of Bronze Age barrows round Stonehenge. The same motives that impel Christians to seek burial near the church were already effective in the Bronze Age, as cemeteries around the Egyptian pyramids and Mesopotamian temples indicate.

South of Brogar a series of five Standing Stones may be remnants of an alignment or even an avenue leading across the narrow isthmus called the Bridge of Brodgar to another sacred enclosure. The *Ring of Stenness* is now a flat-topped mound or platform, encircled by a fosse with a bank outside it and traversed by a causeway on the north-west. On the platform four monoliths stand on the circumference of a circle, some 52 feet in diameter.

The Standing Stones of Callanish, on a promontory projecting into Loch Roag, in Lewis, may belong to the class under discussion. It consists of a circle of 13 stones; it has an average diameter of 37 feet 4 inches. It is approached from the north by an avenue, 270 feet long, composed of 19 stones. A continuance of the avenue south of the circle is suggested by 6 uprights. Lines, each composed of four uprights, project from the circle east and west, so that the whole complex is cruciform in plan.

From the centre of the circle rises a single pillar, the largest stone on the site, 15 feet 6 inches high. It stands in the kerb of a small round cairn. This covers a chamber with entrance passage, the portal of which is formed by the two uprights of the circle that rise immediately to the north of the eastern alignment. The narrow passage opening between these stones on the exterior of the circle leads into the small chamber between a pair of slabs parallel to the portal stones, while opposite them a parallel pair form the portal to a cell in the rear wall. Just outside the circle and abutting against its circumference on the north-east are the remains of another, much denuded cairn.

When the circle was examined by Sir James Matheson about 1855, the chamber had already been opened. No relics were recovered then or subsequently on any part of the site.

BRONZE AGE AND EARLY IRON AGE HOUSES

Prehistoric Dwellings at Jarlshof. It is only from the end of the Bronze Age, and that in Shetland, that any substantial domestic remains survive. Their dating is difficult owing to the divergence in culture of the Orkney and Shetland Islands from the rest of Britain. While even in these northern isles the early Bronze Age can be defined by typical Beakers, neither Food Vessels nor normal Cinerary Urns characterize middle and late Bronze Age graves. Their place is presumably taken respectively by skeletons buried in cist-graves, sometimes with small steatite urns, and by cremations contained either in very small cists or in urns of clay or steatite. Similarly only four metal objects of Middle Bronze Age type are known from Orkney, and none at all from Shetland. Even Late Bronze Age types are missing from the more northern archipelago. But they were manufactured there in one of the dwellings at *Jarlshof.*

These lie near a sandy beach on the west side of the narrow isthmus connecting Sumburgh Head, the southernmost tip of the Shetland

Islands, with the rest of the main island. As at Skara Brae the dwellings owe their preservation to sand dunes that have covered them. But occupation was never interrupted completely as it was after the final desertion of Skara Brae. Successive generations and waves of settlers inhabited the attractive site, and very naturally used the handy stones collected by earlier builders for their own constructions and reconstructions. Hence the dwellings are very incomplete, and the plans are hard to disentangle.

Of the earliest dwelling, uncovered by Childe in 1937, only a few foundation stones survived, but pottery with vaguely neolithic affinities was comparatively plentiful. Dr. A. O. Curle had previously uncovered six dwellings, belonging to several periods, but it is not clear how many were inhabited at one and the same time. Those attributable to the Bronze Age may be termed courtyard houses, and illustrate a quite different conception to the interconnected but one-roomed dwellings at Skara Brae. There, the cluster of single apartments, all interconnected so as to be literally under one midden, if not under one roof, would be suitable for a single clan or "great family", all of whose members co-operated consciously as kinsmen. The Jarlshof houses each seem adapted to a single natural family, owning individually such articles as querns and the beasts that shared their dwelling.

Yet the whole cluster was apparently surrounded by a common wall, constructed just like a dry-stone dyke today. Very little of it is left, but the surviving section includes a sheep gate, precisely like those left in such walls in any part of Highland Britain today.

Typically a courtyard house is made up of five cells grouped symmetrically round the "court", which contained the principal hearth and may have been open. The cells were presumably roofed by corbelling. That in the rear wall opposite the door may be 10 feet long and 6 feet 6 inches deep, and perhaps served as a stable. The smaller cells on either side of the court in that case served the human members of the household as living and sleeping rooms.

This general plan is best exemplified in dwelling I, but even this has been much altered. The original door opened on to a flagged passage on the south-west. On the opposite side of this passage is a small round chamber with a rectangular recess in its left wall. Beside this Dr. Curle found a trough quern and rubber still in position as they are now. They had apparently been used for preparing clay for pot-making. A heap of peat ash found beyond the quern may illustrate the fuel used in the potter's kiln. When this house was built, its owners relied for their equipment entirely on stone and bone, employing quartz instead of flint and manufacturing a great variety of curious implements of slate.

Subsequently a bronze-smith arrived at Jarlshof and made Dwelling I his smithy. The original door was blocked, and a new entrance contrived in the east end of the stall at what had been the back of the house. The flagged passage and the chamber beyond it became a dump for broken moulds. The forge was set up in the court. Here Dr. Curle found in position the stock of clay used by the smith and the quern in which he prepared it. The moulds for casting were built up from this clay round a pattern in an ingenious manner. When completed and dried, the empty mould was set mouth upright in a pit full of sand, which was actually found beside the hearth, and the molten metal poured in. To extract each casting the mould had to be broken, and its fragments were then thrown into the disused passage. The fragments, pieced together, show that the smith was trained in the Irish school, and produced swords, axes and knives of types current in Ireland and Highland Britain in the Late Bronze Age. The copper might be obtained from local ores, but tin, if bronze were really used, must have been imported from Cornwall, while the charcoal for the furnace must have been made from imported wood unless sufficient drift-wood were available.

Dwellings II and V belong to the same period and type. The court of No. V contained in its final form a central hearth, while a quern with rubbing stone lay in a cell on the right. Previously this structure had served as a stable for a beast that may later have been transferred to a court opposite the door. Under the slabs that formed the bottom of the hearth was found a greasy deposit filling a dished area. In the original west wall had been built the atlas vertebra of a whale in such a way that its neural ring formed a loop to which a beast could be tethered. The creature's hindquarters would then be over the dished area, evidently designed for the collection of manure.

Only the ghost of the Bronze Age plan can now be discerned in Dwelling III; for two later and more rounded huts had been built over the original courtyard house. But its original hearth is still in position. Two stone boxes, found full of animal bones, in the doorway of the left-hand cells are somewhat later but still probably of Bronze Age date.

After the site had lain deserted and roofless for a time, during which a deep deposit of sand and rubbish had accumulated on its floor, any protruding stones of the original walls were removed and re-used in the construction of a large roughly circular hut with a diameter of some 25 feet. It was provided with a central hearth and under it is a tunnel-like passage or souterrain. This was entered by a door on the south over the door of the original courtyard house. Still later a larger round house was built on the site at a higher level, the walls of the second being denuded to make room and provide material for the third. To it, too, belongs a souterrain. This was entered through a door in the east wall, blocked by a stone slab that has been left in position. It would give access to a short stair descending to a narrow gallery, 11 feet long, and roofed by lintels only 3 feet above the foundations of its walls.

Dwellings IV and VI are both remains of round houses like the later versions of No. III. The souterrain of VI is intact. It is a narrow passage, only 2 feet wide and 2 feet high, that leads downwards for 20 feet to a subterranean chamber, 6 feet square. Its roof is supported by four pillars, but is raised thereby only 2 feet 8 inches above its floor of pure sand.

The relics from these round houses include none of the slate tools so common in the courtyard houses and indeed very few stone tools at all. Instead a little iron slag was found in one. They belong in fact to a new archæological period, the Iron Age, and to new people whose tastes in pottery were as different from those of the Bronze Age as were their architectural traditions. The iron they used was smelted at Wiltrow, on an exposed hill overlooking the Jarlshof isthmus from the north, where fierce gales would provide a natural blast.

The new round houses appear to have been of the "wheel" type. In all of them there are traces of radial piers or slabs projecting inwards from the encompassing wall, like the spokes of a wheel, as if to divide the circular space into voussoir-shaped compartments. The true purpose of these "spokes" was not, however, primarily divisional, but structural, to support the roof. In England, where timber was available, the wooden rafters of round houses were supported by concentric rings of posts. Slabs on edge and radial piers were substitutes for posts in a treeless region. How the roofs were constructed can best be inferred from other buildings at the site.

The most conspicuous prehistoric structure at Jarlshof today is a broch of somewhat later date than the four round houses just described. It is a badly preserved representative of a class of defensive construction dealt with fully on pp. 43-50. It was provided on the west side with a large oval courtyard. Only the landward half of the courtyard wall remains, built in the same sophisticated masonry and including an intramural cell.

After the abandonment of the broch a large round house was built in the landward arc of the courtyard. Like the broch, this was provided with a scarcement course, the roof probably being of timber. This superstructure was replaced in a secondary phase by a heavier roof supported by eight or nine free standing piers of masonry, of which only five survive. The piers divided the interior of the dwelling into a series of radial stone-paved compartments provided with aumbries or cupboards in the main house wall.

Subsequently this round house was half demolished to make way for two wheel houses, the best preserved examples of their class in Scotland. The earlier of these measures between 35 and 40 feet in diameter and was entered through a semi-circular porch adjacent to the broch tower. This latter structure, however, had been robbed of stone in the building of these post-broch dwellings and its fabric was in a dangerous state. Falls of masonry must have been frequent and caused damage to the occupants of the wheel house. Consequently the porch entrance was abandoned and a partition wall built across the floor of the dwelling, isolating the section adjacent to the tower. The remaining half was entered through a new doorway in the south end of the partition wall. Apart from the voussoir-like compartments formed by the radial walls arranged like the spokes of a wheel, the most interesting internal feature is a well laid U-shaped stone hearth.

The second and later wheel house in the courtyard is smaller, but is in a better state of preservation, with an internal diameter of 24 feet. It is divided into seven segments by radial walls projecting just far enough to leave an uninterrupted paved area in the centre 12 feet across. The walls stand to a height of some 9 feet, corbelling out so as to carry lintels that span six of the compartments at their tops. The seventh compartment on the north west is lintelled over 5 feet 6 inches above its floor. The passage thus formed contains the original entrance.

The remains of two other wheel houses occur inside the broch and on its east side respectively. In the latter area a series of outhouses was constructed including a byre and storage pits. The wheel houses were inhabited for a considerable length of time, during which windblown sand mounded against the outer walls. On the landward slope of the mound several huts were constructed lying within an enclosure wall. Outside the old courtyard wall and in 9 to 10 feet of windblown sand, a large earth house was constructed, first entered down a stone stairway, but later provided with a sloping entrance passage. Associated finds show that these secondary structures were inhabited as late as the 7-8th centuries A.D.

They were eventually replaced by a Viking settlement, the most complete of its kind yet discovered in the British Isles. Only the walls and foundations of the Norse houses remain, covering an area of almost two acres on the landward slope. The growth of this settlement, however, can be followed from the 9th to the 13th century, and it provides a most interesting picture of life in the Scottish Islands during Viking and later Norse times.

THE IRON AGE AND THE ROMANO-BRITISH PERIOD

An Iron Age did not begin in Scotland before 200 B.C. and perhaps not till after 50, with the advent of several bands of new conquerors. These can be confidently described as Kelts, meaning by that people who spoke a Keltic language. They not only introduced the use of a new industrial metal, but also initiated an agricultural revolution. Iron made efficient metal tools cheap and available to all, so that forest-clearance, drainage, quarrying, and all branches of carpentry could be carried out with greater economy of labour and more extensively than ever before. In the new rural economy settled farming based on plough cultivation, always combined with stock-breeding, gradually replaced the old system of shifting cultivation and pastoralism. At the same time the ploughed fields, left fallow under grass, provided pasture for sheep that had not been available when exhausted plots were allowed to relapse into scrub—save of course in the far north where the wind bared moors had always offered grazing. As a result flocks multiplied, so that plenty of wool was available for a textile industry. Appliances connected with spinning and weaving are prominent on all Iron Age sites and among the new tools made available by cheap iron are shears.

On the other hand cheap metal meant cheap weapons as well as cheap tools and the Kelts were exceedingly bellicose. But horse-drawn chariots were the decisive engines of war, comparable to tanks today. Now chariots and steeds, specially trained to draw them, were excessively costly, the prerogative of chieftains. At the same time such well-armed champions were essential to the safety of the group while their authority was consolidated by their *de facto* monopoly of the decisive armament.

Hence with the Iron Age the whole character of the archæological record changes. Instead of burial cairns, standing stones, and ritual circles, the most conspicuous monuments are defensive constructions, the utility of which we can easily appreciate.

During the Iron Age, prehistory gives place to history. In A.D. 43 England became a Province of the Roman Empire. Forty years later the Roman legions under Agricola—father-in-law of the famous historian, Tacitus—advanced into Scotland and the Roman fleet sailed round the northern coasts of Great Britain. After defeating the "Britons" at Mons Graupius (an unidentified battlefield), Agricola established a frontier held by garrisons stationed at a line of posts between the Forth and Clyde with outposts along a road running from the Forth near Stirling to the Tay above Perth. These garrisons were maintained precariously for some thirty years, but about A.D. 122 were withdrawn behind the new frontier from the Tyne to the Solway, established by the Emperor Hadrian. Some forty years later the Romans advanced again and fortified the Forth-Clyde isthmus with the rampart and ditch known as the Antonine Wall. This was finally abandoned some time between A.D. 180 and 205.

In that interval the area south of the Wall was effectively subject to Rome, but always a frontier province, not a civil province like southern England. The "natives" were left to live their old tribal life in "hill forts" and fortified farms, provided that they paid tribute regularly and did not rob Roman soldiers and merchants. North of the isthmus the natives never long submitted to even that restraint.

Most of the monuments to be described now were occupied, some actually built, during the Roman period, i.e. between A.D. 80 and 205. There is only one class of Iron Age monument certainly erected before and not inhabited after A.D. 83. These are forts defended by gigantic stone walls laced with timbers; in some the timbers in the ramparts have been set on fire producing "vitrified" walls owing to the fusion of the rubble core. The Ministry has in guardianship no certain example of such Gallic forts, so-called from Julius Cæsar's description of a *murus gallicus*. Those monuments that are so protected include "hilltop forts," brochs, fortified farm steadings and a single sculpture executed by the Romans.

HILL-TOP FORTS, though exposed to the full fury of biting winds, were actually fortified villages or "fenced cities" in the words of the Bible. None was a city in the modern sense inhabited by a large proportion of shopkeepers, artisans, clerics and officials. All their "citizens" were working farmers, save, perhaps, for a couple of craftsmen and a chief. They vary greatly in area, and the existing grassy banks give no idea of the really formidable ramparts that once defended them.

The White Caterthun crowns a spur of the Grampians, 975 feet above the sea, overlooking the Esk valley and thus commanding the northern end of Strathmore. The summit was once girt with a mighty stone rampart, enclosing an irregular space over 470 feet long but at most 220 feet wide. The rampart has been completely dismantled and now appears as a shapeless bank of naked rubble. Though it was undoubtedly faced inside and out with built masonry, no trace of face is exposed. Indeed, without excavation it is impossible to decide whether the present belt of stones is a single line of defence or two parallel walls, still less how it was constructed. Quite probably the masonry was laced with timbers in the Gallic style as was that of the "vitrified" fort on Finavon Hill on the opposite side of the Esk Valley.

Traces of a cistern are visible within the enclosure, which on the analogy of Finavon should mark the mouth of a well cut into the living rock for a depth of perhaps 20 feet. If the analogy with Finavon be valid, this citadel should have been built in pre-Roman times, perhaps as early as 200 B.C., while its destruction, like that of Finavon, might be attributed to Agricola's legions.

Outside and below the stone rampart are traces of a defensive ditch with a counterscarp bank outside it. Then 100 feet to 250 feet further down the slope is another line of defence with an annexe on the north-east. This outer rampart looks like an earthen bank with a ditch beyond it. A considerable stretch of the imagination is needed to realize that this was once a formidable obstacle, which a stout timber palisade once undoubtedly made it. But excavation is required to determine its structure and its relation to the stone-walled citadel. Its inclusion would bring the total defensible area up to 1,300 feet by 850 feet.

A sub-rectangular construction inside the citadel is obviously later than the stone rampart, but otherwise of uncertain age.

The Brown Caterthun crowns an eminence three-quarters of a mile north-east of the foregoing and separated therefrom by a glen. The defences appear to consist of four concentric banks and ditches, interrupted by frequent gaps and causeways. This peculiarity has suggested comparison with the causewayed camps of southern England and France which were certainly constructed in the Neolithic Age! The validity of this comparison has not been tested by excavation.

It is just as likely that this fort is the successor of the White Caterthun, erected after the withdrawal of the Roman legions, and that its defences represent two periods. The innermost and third banks could belong to an earlier, the second and outermost banks to a later phase. The latter are both supplemented by ditches. In any case the visitor should remember that the low grassy banks now visible are only the last remnants of really imposing ramparts.

BROCHS.—The essential feature of any broch is a circular wall of neat masonry, 10 feet to 16 feet thick, pierced by a single tunnel-like entrance and enclosing a space 20 feet to 30 feet across. Within the thickness of the wall there must be two to four corbelled cells from one of which, on the left as one enters, a staircase begins to mount clockwise within the walls. Another cell should command one end of the hole in which the bar, fastening the door, slid.

But sometimes at least this was only the ground floor, and formed the foundation for two concentric walls set close together, the inner vertical, the outer externally battered. These were held together at vertical intervals of about 5 feet by horizontal slabs bonded into both walls. The slabs thus form the pavements for narrow galleries interrupted only to make way for the stair that continues to wind up between the walls from the ground floor. There is no aperture in the outer wall; four narrow slits, interrupted only by the gallery floors, run up the interior wall.

One broch, *Mousa*, still stands as a tower 43 feet 6 inches high. At least six others rise, or are known to have risen, to heights of over 25 feet. Some 23 more stand high enough to show at least one wall gallery above the ground floor. Of the rest, that are more than grass grown mounds—only some 25 in all—the massive ground-floor wall alone survives. Yet it has been generally accepted that all brochs were once towers, comparable in height to Mousa. That view was challenged in 1947 by Sir Lindsay Scott and can no longer be regarded as accepted by all students.

Most excavated brochs appear to have been occupied for several centuries, during which the features above described and still more the internal arrangements of the ground-floor had been more or less drastically altered. Still, comparative study reveals common features that may be regarded as primary. In the centre of the ground-floor court stood a rectangular hearth. A ring of posts or stone uprights round it is supposed to have supported the ends of radial beams connected with a verandah roof all round the central court. The outer ends of the rafters would have rested on a ledge or scarcement running round the enclosing wall some six feet from the ground. A second scarcement much higher up exists at Mousa and *Dun Telve*. There is normally a well or cistern in the court that may be reached by a descending stair.

The central court with its "verandah roof" was the principal living room of the edifice. No one imagines that the tower, if any, was closed in at its top by woodwork or corbelled masonry, and the "galleries" are too narrow to be more than structural. Brochs are always built of quarry-dressed blocks with small stones ingeniously inserted as pinnings between the joints.

Most brochs stand in a defensible enclosure partly protected by a wall, built in the same style of masonry as the "tower" and sometimes comprising stairs or intramural cells. Advantage has been taken of any natural features, so that a cliff or a river may replace part of the encircling wall. Within the enclosure remains of huts are usually

Plate 11. *Meigle Museum, Angus*

Plate 12. *Sueno's Stone, Morayshire*

Plate 13. *Kildrummy Castle, Aberdeenshire*

Plate 14. *The great 'donjon', Bothwell Castle, Lanarkshire*

visible, but these are generally of inferior construction and sometimes plainly secondary.

Brochs are densely concentrated in Shetland (51 to 95), Orkney (44 to 105), Caithness and Sutherland (over 200), the Hebrides and Skye (34). These districts with the adjacent parts of Ross and western Inverness constitute the main broch area. Beyond it are 4 or 5 on Mull, one on Tiree, 3 on Islay, one on Lismore, one in Strath Glass and then in the Lowlands, two near Stirling, two on the Gala Water and one on the Lammermuirs. Within the main area brochs are thickest along the coasts but extend far inland up fertile straths. They are invariably placed on good arable land. But those on the coast frequently overlook sheltered inlets, convenient bases for piracy and fishing. On suitable land, brochs were often built very close together, so that there may be three within a radius of 500 yards. Such proximity is not altogether easy to reconcile with the theory that brochs were the castles of independent chieftains, each with his retainers dwelling in the shadow of their lord's tower.

What the relics from brochs do indicate is an absorbing pre-occupation with farming and a highly developed textile industry. Iron and bronze were worked within the enceintes. Trade or piracy secured to the broch people even in Orkney a few Roman coins, Roman vases and even Roman saucepans. Several lines of evidence converge to show that the brochs were built by invaders, come by sea from south-western England, who had just colonized the extreme north of Britain at the beginning of our era and had been able to send parties to occupy tracts round Stirling and Galashiels before A.D. 140. While the invaders preserved the industrial techniques, notably in spinning and weaving, that they had developed in the south, they have left no trace of the splendid "Keltic art," which their ancestors had applied to the decoration of even domestic pottery in the last centuries before our era.

No less than nine brochs are under the Ministry's guardianship and each shows some individual peculiarities. But only a few can be described at all fully.

The Broch of Mousa stands on the shore of a small rocky island, yet was defended on the landward side by a wall, now much dilapidated.

It has often been taken as the most typical broch, so only divergences from the ideal norm need be mentioned. The solid "ground-floor" wall is exceptionally high, 12 feet 4 inches. Immediately above the present entrance there was once an entrance passage, but its mouth was built up in 1919. Again the entrance to the stairhouse cells is approximately on a level with the floor of this upper passage and some 6 feet above the primary floor, but just below the second scarcement. Below it are three intramural cells entered by descending steps. At the bottom of the court is a rock-cut cistern that is doubtless original. On the other hand the present hearth, a radial wall, and a low wall, concentric with and inside the main wall, seem to be secondary additions to the original plan.

According to Egil's Saga an eloping couple from Norway took refuge in the broch about A.D. 900, and a similar incident about 1153 is recorded in the Orkneyinga Saga.

The Broch of Clickhimin stands on an islet (now a promontory) in the Loch of the same name, ¾ of a mile south-west of Lerwick, and was originally connected with the land only by a causeway, 7 feet 6 inches wide. Access to this was controlled by a gateway, now dilapidated, on the threshold of which are two depressions in the form of human feet. (Such impressions are traditionally connected with the inauguration ceremonies of both Keltic and Teutonic kings). The wall encircling the islet is reached after 42 feet and is pierced by a passage, reduced by a jamb to barely 4 feet in width. Immediately in front of this inner gate is a short section of wall, built in true broch style and comprising an intramural cell and stair. It, too, is pierced by a door only 4 feet 3 inches high. To reach the door of the broch proper, one must then turn left and traverse a corridor beneath its walls.

The plan of the broch is confused by many additions and alterations both inside and outside. These include secondary entrances on the north-north-west and the north-east. In the enclosure outside are ruinous remains of several buildings.

The Broch of Gurness, in Orkney, crowns a rocky headland, some 15 feet high, facing Rousay at the narrowest point of Eynhallow Sound. When excavations were started in 1930, the site was marked by a low grassy mound, and no indication at all of the great encircling fosse was superficially visible. But the tower turns out to stand over 10 feet high, though it has been much altered during prolonged occupation.

Originally there were long galleries opening off the entrance passage in the thickness of the wall at ground level. The cell from which the stairway starts is situated above these in a second storey of the massive wall. In the court stood a hearth, while an opening beside it gave access to a stair, which leads down to a subterranean well-chamber, where a natural spring fills a rock-cut basin.

These original features have been partly masked by later structures, erected when part of the tower's walls had collapsed. Then cubicles of flagstone were run up in the court, and a new stair was built against the inner wall face, presumably to give access to the upper storeys of the cubicles and to a rampart walk. Near the level of the present wall top Craw found a Viking shield-buckle, perhaps part of the furniture of a burial inserted in the mound when the interior of the abandoned tower had been filled up with rubbish and debris. Save perhaps on the seaward side, where much erosion has taken place, the tower was protected by a great rock-cut fosse, 8 feet to 17 feet wide, with a stout stone rampart outside it. Subsequently this rampart was removed and replaced by a series of bastion walls that rise from the bed of the original fosse, while two outer ramparts and ditches were added.

The entrance gates and causeways lie to the east, parallel to the present sea cliff. A gatehouse beyond the primary fosse appears to be part of the original defences.

Huts and cubicles of all kinds were built and rebuilt between the base of the tower and the ramparts, and encroached on to the line of the primary fosse when that was abandoned. The site was inhabited even when deserted by the broch-builders. Early in Viking times a curious building resembling a shamrock leaf in plan was run up in rather inferior masonry. This had to be removed, to allow of the exposure of earlier structures, but has been re-erected west of the broch. Still later may be a long-house, the normal farmhouse of the Viking period, similar to those at Jarlshof and Birsay (pp. 118, 108), of which only one end is preserved.

The excavators recovered part of a Roman wine jar, much hand-made native pottery, textile implements, dice and other objects of bone and querns of the broch period, ornaments belonging to the subsequent "Dark Age", and others introduced by the Viking colonists from Norway.

Mid Howe Broch, on the opposite shore of Eynhallow Sound but further north-west along the coast of Rousay, occupies the extremity of a long rocky promontory that rises precipitously between two clefts or "geos". The base of the promontory was cut off by a rock-cut ditch, 6 feet deep and 9 feet wide, and a massive wall, behind which there was once an inner ditch. Access to the enclosure is provided by a causeway along the edge of Stenchna Geo. It leads to a gateway in the wall, which was continued, beyond this interruption, along the edge of the geo seaward. Just within the gate this section of the wall is pierced by a water gate, from which nine rock-cut steps lead down towards the sea. So the geo must have served as a boat-harbour and landing place.

The entrance to the broch itself is on the seaward side, as far as possible from the gateway through the rampart. The tower still stands 14 feet high in places, but much of its outer wall is missing. As at Gurness, there is a narrow gallery in the thickness of the wall at ground level, and the stair begins in the storey above this in a cell,

5 feet 9 inches from the floor of the court. The gallery to which it gives access is poorly preserved, and partly blocked by a high level intramural cell which may be a secondary insertion.

The court is occupied by a number of odd constructions in which upright slabs and corbelling are combined in an ingenious way. Most were probably built at a time when the broch walls showed a tendency to collapse, which necessitated the blocking of most of the ground-floor gallery. A stone box with a tightly fitting lid must, however, belong to the original plan. It contains a spring of fresh water.

The fortified enceinte, considerably diminished by the encroachment of the sea on the north, is built over with cubicles and chambers. Most have certainly been erected after the broch and its enceinte wall; some indeed are built over the inner ditch. In several chambers stone furniture, reminiscent of Skara Brae, survives; in one are remains of an iron-smelting furnace, beside which a large earthenware jar was found sunk in the ground.

The broch was excavated by W. G. Grant between 1930 and 1934. The excavations brought to light a series of relics illustrative of the life of the broch period. They include saddle and rotary querns, textile appliances, vessels of whale-bone and of native pottery, personal ornaments and fragments of a bronze saucepan of Roman manufacture. Though iron was smelted at the site, hardly any objects of that metal survived. No remains of the Viking period were found.

Mid Howe is the central member of a group of three brochs, all within a distance of 500 yards. The other two appear as mere grassy mounds, as was Mid Howe till 1930. The great Neolithic burial place described on p. 16, adjoins the broch within the same enclosure.

Two tall brochs in *Glenelg*, and *Dun Carloway* in Lewis, offer no features that require additions to the general explanation given on p. 43.

Edin's Hall is one of five brochs in the Lowlands and in diameter is by far the largest broch known, though its plan is normal. It stands on the edge of a broad terrace that slopes up gently on the south to Cockburn's Law, which is crowned by a hill-top fort, but falls away precipitously northward to the Whitadder, some 200 feet below. The edge of the gorge was defended by a double stone wall, most of which has fallen down the declivity. On the naturally exposed southern side these walls are continued by more imposing defences, which appear now as two high banks with deep ditches outside each. Gaps and causeways in the south-west corner mark one entry to the enceinte. A second entrance on the east leads to a broad road, flanked with stone walls, which after 110 feet is constricted by an inner gate.

The west end of the enceinte is cut off by a transverse wall or bank. Beyond this are remains of a further wall, joining the main rampart on the north-west and turning eastward after a gap, but never reaching the main rampart again on the north. It seems instead to abut against the outer wall of the broch. The latter thus stands in a sort of inner bailey.

The broch is no less than 55 feet in diameter inside. The wall is 15 feet to 20 feet thick and built in normal broch masonry, but much denuded. It contains five cells. These, like the entrance passage, are now roofless but the commencement of the corbelling may be observed. The cells are very large and four have been divided by piers, inserted secondarily, as if to afford extra support to the corbelled roof. Eight steps of the intramural stairway survive, but naturally no trace of galleries.

In the outer enceinte are ruinous remains of several stone-walled, curvilinear buildings of varying sizes. At least superficially they are strikingly like the similar structures round the broch of Clickhimin (p. 46). Excavations were conducted on the site by Mr. Turnbull shortly before 1879, but they did not disclose how the several ramparts and buildings are related to one another and to the broch, nor produce any significant relics.

"Galleried Dun" and "Semibroch" are terms applied to miscellaneous structures defended by walls the masonry of which agrees in some significant features with that of brochs, but which enclose larger or less regular areas and are never more than two storeys high.

On the *Ness of Burgi*, in Shetland, stands the only—but far from typical—representative of this class under the Ministry's guardianship. The Ness is the southern tip of the peninsula of Scatness on the west side of the Voe of Sumburgh, on the opposite shore of which lies Jarlshof with its broch. The flat-topped promontory is cut off at its neck by two deep ditches with a rampart between them. This rampart is pierced near its centre by a single gate. Beyond the inner ditch and roughly parallel to it rises a length of massive wall, now about 75 feet long and from 21 feet to 18 feet 6 inches thick. It terminates on the cliff at its south-west end, part of which has actually fallen into the ocean, but on the north-east the wall seems to have been finished off more than 20 feet short of the cliff edge.

This curious wall is pierced by a tunnel, like the entrance to a broch, roofed 4 feet above its floor. Just within the door-jambs an aperture on the left gives access to an intramural cell, 6 feet 6 inches long and originally roofed by corbelling. In the southern section of the wall were two cells. The walls of one have largely fallen over the cliff.

The other is entered from the inner face of the wall by a passage parallel to the main entrance. The bar for fastening the door could be controlled both from this cell and from that first described. No structures survive in the area between the wall and the sea cliff. Two hearths, belonging to consecutive periods, were found within the southern cell.

SMALL FORTS. Most of the smaller enclosures generally labelled "fort" or "camp" are probably fortified steadings rather than military works or castles. Such are hardly ever situated on hill-tops, but generally on a spur some way below the summit, and not always in an obviously strategic position, but usually on or just above good arable land. Wells or other internal provision for water are not superficially visible. Such earthworks are common in Fife and still more in the area between the two walls. Outside the areas occupied by the Romans they are exceptional. They display much variety in plan and location, and in many cases can be seen to represent more than one period of occupation.

Castle Law, Glencorse, is typical of a large class in the Lothians and the Border counties. It is one of a series along the southern flanks of the Pentlands, overlooking the modern road from Edinburgh to Biggar, which follows the route of a Roman road. The earthwork occupies the top of a low knoll on a spur from the main hill that bears its name, and overlooks the mouth of Glencorse, a natural route through the Pentland range. This summit is encircled by two banks and two ditches that prove to belong to two structural periods. The inner bank is now scarcely visible, but marks the line of a stoney garth rampart laced with timbers. It encloses a space some 280 feet long and at most 120 feet wide which has not been excavated.

There are gaps, suggestive of entrances, on the west, the south and the east. The western gap marks the site of a barbican gate framed by four stout posts, which had been renewed more than once; the sockets for these posts were found in 1932. The fairway through the gate was 7 feet 6 inches wide.

Below this rampart ran a rock-cut ditch, some 8 feet wide and over six feet deep. Opposite the west gate the ends of the ditch overlap, so that in traversing the causeway any visitor or assailant would have to turn left to reach the gate.

In the second period this ditch was abandoned. A new rampart was constructed further down the slope, and this overran the filled-in end of the old ditch north of the west causeway. The new rampart was faced externally with timbers, set close together but sloping slightly inwards in a continuous trench. Below this rampart runs a second rock-cut ditch, 10 feet wide and 6 feet deep, with a counterscarp bank beyond it. Defences like the foregoing were probably repeated round

other similar earthworks, all too small to accommodate anything but a big farm.

But Castlelaw exhibits one exceptional, and so far unique, feature. About the time the second rampart was constructed a souterrain or earth-house was built in the north-west end of the disused inner ditch. For that purpose the original V-shaped excavation was widened and its rock floor levelled out. The crumbling basalt faces of the enlarged trench were lined with masonry walls that once supported rafters, which have decayed, and a few stone lintels which collapsed. One lintel is still lying on the floor, but the roof has been replaced by a concrete float at approximately the original level. It has been turfed over, as the original roof probably was. The walls are composed largely of water-worn boulders fetched from the valley and are founded on large blocks set on edge.

The subterranean gallery thus formed is 72 feet long. It is entered by four rock-cut steps descending from the old west causeway across the former ditch. The door at the foot was originally only 1 foot 3 inches wide and framed with wooden jambs. The rock-cut sockets for these were found, but they have been replaced by modern masonry supporting a door of less constricted proportions. Beyond the door the passage, still low and narrow, descends gently, but after 35 feet begins to widen out to a long chamber 6 feet 6 inches wide and at least 5 feet 6 inches high. An aumbry in the right hand wall of the passage, 21 feet from the door, would have served conveniently to hold a lamp.

So far the gallery conforms to the general plan of other souterrains as described below. But this example boasts another less usual feature. A narrow doorway, 3 feet 4 inches high, in the right hand wall gives access to a circular chamber built in an excavation quarried in the rock. Its walls stand today little more than 6 feet high, but already corbel inwards. The whole space save for a smoke-hole must have been covered with a beehive roof, over which earth and turf would have been piled.

Opposite the entrance the floor of a recessed cupboard is preserved at the present wall-head. In the middle of the rock floor is a shallow excavation. This was the base of a hearth used by a metal-worker. It was found full of iron slag, while a bloom of iron and a bar or ingot of bronze were found in the chamber. Other relics recovered include Roman glass and pottery of the second century A.D., an enamelled brooch, and a bronze buckle of Keltic style but probably made in the Rhineland in the second century, as well as a rotary quern, a lignite spindle-whorl and a very few fragments of hand-made, native pottery.

The souterrain and the later defences accordingly existed about A.D. 200. The primary occupation is not likely to be separated from the second by any great interval of desertion. Was the fort, perhaps, first built in the period of Roman withdrawal between A.D. 120 and 140?

The comparatively strong defences of this farm steading and its exposed but strategic position are indicative of the turbulence and insecurity of the periods during which it was occupied. In the second phase at least its inhabitants were obstinately self-sufficient, since they smelted iron on the spot instead of buying it in a hill-top fort such as Traprain Law, which is visible from the site.

SOUTERRAINS. Save for its position the underground gallery at Castlelaw is typical of a puzzling class of monuments, termed "souterrains" in Ireland and France, but "earth-houses" or "weems" in Scotland, and "fogous" in Cornwall. They are very numerous in Ireland, but in Great Britain are virtually confined to Cornwall, Strathmore, Aberdeenshire, and the counties further north. In Scotland there are a few in Fife and the Lothians, but they seem unknown in the west save in the Hebrides and Sutherland. A souterrain is normally an underground gallery as at Castlelaw. The beehive annex noted there can be matched in Cornwall and in Angus where the roof is intact.

Scottish souterrains are only exceptionally found connected with any superficially visible remains of above-ground buildings, but are nearly always on arable land, sometimes indeed in modern farmyards. These underground cellars or funk-holes were certainly never built in isolation. They were attached to, and probably entered from, a normal overground dwelling-house, which, being built of wood, has left no superficial marks. Accordingly the term "earth-house" suggesting regular habitation, is a misnomer. A souterrain must have served as a convenient refuge, where women and children could defend themselves and their treasures during a brief raid for slaves and cattle. They could also be utilized for the storage of provisions.

Presumably such refuges or cellars belonged to well-to-do farmers, perhaps even petty chieftains. They thus afford evidence for the existence of open farm steadings or hamlets, of which no other trace is likely to survive, since modern ploughing or farm-buildings will have destroyed even the sockets of the posts that sustained the vanished walls.

One souterrain near Crichton in Midlothian is partly built of stones taken from an abandoned Roman fort. That at Castlelaw, we have seen, goes back to the second century. Even first century relics were found in another at Tealing. But the very primitive souterrains attached to the round huts at Jarlshof (p. 36) which are older than the broch, must be older than the Christian era. In that case the earliest, as well as the most primitive, souterrains in Scotland have been found in the most northern county.

Tealing Earth-house, is a long curved gallery, some 80 feet long and 7 feet 6 inches to 8 feet 6 inches wide. It was probably roofed over with wooden beams some 6 feet above the floor, which is mostly formed of the native trap rock. Access to the gallery was obtained by a steeply inclined passage, 3 feet to 3 feet 8 inches wide and through a door of which the jambs and sill-stones alone survive. Just within this door a stone on the right is carved with cup-and-ring marks, identical in form and technique with the Bronze Age carving described on p. 27. Cup-and-ring marked stones have been used in building other earth-houses in Angus. It is by no means clear whether these were stones carved much earlier in the Bronze Age and then re-used by the Iron Age builders of earth-houses, or indicate the survival of Bronze Age traditions, and therefore of some of the Bronze Age people, into the Iron Age. Near the inner end of the gallery a second pair of jambs define the entrance to a small inner chamber.

When the site was discovered in 1861, a circular cobbled area was noticed on the surface of the ground in the angle between the descending entrance passage and the chamber proper. It certainly belongs to the overground dwelling, to which the earth-house was attached as a refuge or cellar. Ten querns (hand-mills for grinding corn), some iron objects, and fragments of Roman pottery were found in the gallery itself.

Ardestie Earth-house, discovered in 1949, provides the clearest example in Angus of surface dwellings attached to a souterrain. These are four huts, circular or ovoid in shape, carefully paved, and with large boulders forming the lower courses of their walls. The souterrain itself, a curved gallery like that at Tealing, is 80 feet long and 7 feet wide. Structurally it is a trench faced with boulders and split flagstones, the latter corbelled inwards to carry a roof of huge slabs. Beneath the paving of the souterrain a drain was constructed, not initially but no doubt as soon as it was realized that the souterrain, sunk into boulder clay, annually became a reservoir for trapped surface water. At a date not far removed from A.D. 200 the souterrain was carefully dismantled, but the site continued to be occupied by the souterrain people. Finds include a cup-and-ring marked boulder, querns, several pieces of native pottery, and the bung from a Roman amphora.

Carlungie Earth-house, one mile from Ardestie and likewise discovered in 1949, also had attached surface dwellings, but the traces of them were not so obvious. Here, too, occupation continued after the souterrain itself was abandoned. But the Carlungie souterrain, about 150 feet long, is more complex than that at Ardestie. In addition to the main entrance, there are three narrower entrances, one of which leads through an underground chamber which was used as a workshop. Finds were more numerous and more varied than at Ardestie, and at both sites the inhabitants were men who grew corn, kept cattle, sheep and pigs, and engaged to some extent in hunting and fishing. Within 150 yards of the Carlungie souterrain, another souterrain (Carlungie II) was discovered and identified in 1949.

Rennibister Earth-House illustrates a variety proper to the Orkney Islands. It lies in a modern farmyard, and was discovered in 1926, when the weight of a threshing machine broke the roof. It consists of an oval chamber, 11 feet 3 inches long by 8 feet 6 inches wide, but only 5 feet high at the centre. Four pillars helped to support the roof. The chamber is now entered through a hatch in the modern concrete roof, but the original entrance was along a passage, 11 feet 6 inches long but only 2 feet wide and 2 feet 3 inches high. One could apparently crawl down into this tunnel without the aid of steps where there is now a grille. When discovered, the floor of the chamber was littered with the bones of people of all ages and both sexes.

Grain "Gallery Grave," discovered in 1827, is situated on a disused airfield just outside Kirkwall. The chamber resembles that at Rennibister in plan and in the use of pillars, but is 13 feet long and 6 feet 6 inches high, though only 6 feet wide. It is entered by a descending passage, 2 feet 6 inches wide and originally 3 feet high, but the trench cut down the centre of the passage floor is probably recent. The passage is reached by a stairway that enters it from the side a couple of feet from its end. No relics are known to have been found in this structure.

Rispain Camp, Wigtownshire. Rispain Camp comprises an area of nearly an acre on the top of a low ridge, enclosed by two banks and ditches. The inner bank has been almost entirely obliterated by agricultural operations, but it is still visible even at the north-eastern side where was the original entrance. The inner ditch and outer bank are both of imposing dimensions but the outer ditch is scarcely now visible. The shape of this camp, which is almost a rectangle, has suggested a Roman origin, but its precise situation makes such an attribution unlikely, and the shape may be due merely to the configuration of the ground. The camp should be regarded as of Iron Age date.

THE ROMAN OCCUPATION

Something has already been said above (p. 41) about the Roman invasion and its effect upon the constructions of the native folk. But the Romans have left important monuments of their own in Scotland. As might be expected in this wild frontier region, these are purely military in character. Indeed, civil life can hardly be said to have existed, unless in the "bazaars" or cantonments that adjoined the military posts. Roman remains in Scotland may be classified under four heads:—roads; marching camps; forts; and the frontier works on the Forth-Clyde isthmus. Many Roman forts have been identified in Scotland, and a number have been more or less explored. Of these latter, the most famous are Birrens on the Solway, the Roman *Blatobulgium*, and Newstead, *Trimontium*, on the Tweed. The excavation of Newstead, by the late Dr. James Curle in 1905-10, formed a landmark in the history of classical archæology in western Europe. At present (1960) a legionary fortress is being explored at Inchtuthill on the Tay. The northmost permanent fort so far known is at Cardean near Meigle in Angus. Thence a line of marching camps extends northwards at least as far as the Spey.

The most important Roman work remaining in Scotland is the Antonine Wall. The frontier line betwixt Forth and Clyde was first marked out by Julius Agricola in the year A.D. 80. Some of his *praesidia*, small entrenched posts, have been identified. In A.D. 143 the legate Lollius Urbicus, acting for the Emperor Antoninus Pius, laid out a permanent frontier on the Agricolan line. This consisted of a wall made of sods on a stone foundation, except in the eastern section, where the wall is of clay. In front was a ditch, deep and wide, and in rear a military way. The garrison was disposed in some twenty forts, mostly built of turf, though at least two had stone walls. The whole barrier is 36 miles long. It was held, but with at least two interruptions, till about the end of the second century. One of the Antonine Wall forts, *Rough Castle*, near Bonnybridge, Stirlingshire and three outstanding lengths of the Wall in Stirlingshire are in the custody of the Ministry. These are meantime the only Roman constructions in Scotland in its charge.

THE DARK AGES

The period from the 5th to 10th centuries was a troubled time in Scottish history when the Scots, Picts, Britons and Angles, and later, Scandinavians, were striving for the mastery of Central and Southern Scotland. As a description of the Early Christian Monuments and Pictish Symbol Stones is given elsewhere it is only necessary here to refer to the hill-fort at Dunadd in Argyll, reputed to be the ancient capital of Dalriada, the primitive Kingdom of the Scots.

Dunadd. This fort, situated on the hill of Dunadd, rising to 160 feet above the flat expanse of Crinan Moss is one of the very few hill forts mentioned in the early annals of our country. There is no reason to doubt that it was the Dunadd or Duinatt besieged in A.D. 683 by Feacher Fadha, chief of Cinnel Baeden, allied with Bredei, King of the Picts, in an attempt to deliver Dalriada from the thraldom of the Britons and Angles. The only other historical event relating to Dunadd was its siege and capture by Angus MacFergus, King of the Picts, in A.D. 736. It would appear to have lost much of its importance after 843 A.D. when Forteviot became the capital of the united Picts and Scots.

The site of Dunadd was well chosen for the capital or chief fortress of the Kingdom, being situated at the junction of the two provinces into which Dalriada was divided—Lorn and Kintyre; it stood in the way of invasion by the only easy access to the Kingdom from the east.

The fort consists of a fortified hill summit from which five walled enclosures loop out, their size being governed by the natural features of the hill. An outermost rampart of which only vestiges remain can be seen on the edge of a broad natural terrace some 30 yards outside the lowest enclosure wall. In the lowest and largest enclosure, divided into two sections and entered from the south through a natural cleft, the well of the fort may be seen at the north end. In the walled enclosure below the summit is a flat rock surface bearing three rock carvings which are regarded as having a connection with the inauguration of the Kings of Dalriada. These consist of a stone basin, the imprint of a human foot pecked out in the rock and between these a fine outlined figure of a boar.

Relics recovered from the excavations by J. H. Craw in 1929 confirmed the occupation of Dunadd from the beginning of the 6th to the middle of the 9th centuries, with an earlier occupation dating at least from early in the Iron Age.

THE CELTIC PERIOD

Regarded as a whole, the monuments of medieval Scotland derive much of their interest from the fact that they represent the interaction of two very different civilizations—that of the ancient Celtic inhabitants, and that of the Anglo-Norman intruders who, in the twelfth century, under the patronage of the Canmore dynasty, began to settle in earnest along the eastern plains.

Although the Celtic states of early Scotland have long since disappeared as corporate entities, the abiding heritage of Celtic art remains as one of the most valuable elements in the cultural make-up of Scottish nationhood today. Reaching its efflorescence in the so-called Dark Ages, this art has bequeathed to posterity upon Scottish soil some of the loveliest monuments of any period now to be seen in Western Europe. To the dim border line between prehistoric and historical times belong the remarkable sculptured stones with their unexplained symbolical forms which are to be found in many a quiet country churchyard, or standing all lonely out in the open fields, throughout that part of Scotland lying north of Forth and east of Drumalban—as the central mountain backbone was called in Celtic times. This was the ancient kingdom of the Picts, and the whole corpus of ideographic art is therefore not unrightly known as Pictish symbolism. A number of the best of these stones are now in the custody of the Ministry of Works. The oldest class are found principally betwixt Dee and Spey. In these, the weird symbolic forms are incised upon more or less unshapen boulders. In the second class, the stones are more carefully dressed, and the symbols are carved in relief, and often highly enriched with beautiful plaitwork or other forms of Celtic ornament. Moreover, they are now accompanied by a Christian cross of Celtic design, similarly enriched. Figure sculpture and animal forms, wrought with rare verve, are often present. In some of the later stones vine-scrolls and other motives of Romanesque derivation, indicating Northumbrian influence, make their appearance. Most of these elaborately decorated slabs, often of extreme beauty, occur in the sandstone basins of Strathmore and Moray, where the material is more suitable than the intractable granites and schists of Mar and Buchan.

In a few cases, alike in stones of Class I and Class II, ogham inscriptions occur. The ogham alphabet, found also on Dark Age monuments of Wales, Cornwall and Ireland, is a system of writing composed of strokes or notches arranged in various combinations upon a stem-line

—often a sharp edge or keel on the stone. Unfortunately, no agreement has yet been reached in the interpretation of our Scottish oghams.

Finally, the third stage of these monuments is reached when the Pictish symbols fall into disuse, and only the Celtic cross, graven on a slab, remains. The most remarkable of these monuments on the eastern side of Scotland is *Sueno's Stone*, at Forres. It is 20 feet high, and the tall cross is accompanied by elaborate figure sculpture. Sometimes whole assemblages of these stones occur on a single site, like the group of 25 now in the Ministry's custody at *Meigle*. Taken altogether, these Celtic sculptured slabs of eastern Scotland form a body of early art of which any nation might feel proud.

West of Drumalban the Celtic cross, following the Irish fashion, more usually occurs free-standing; and here the characteristic art of the sculptured stone survives, in forms becoming ever more debased and mingled with Romanesque and Gothic motives, until as late as the sixteenth century. Many of these late West Highland sculptured grave slabs, or free-standing crosses, such as those at *Kilmory Knap*, are of much beauty.

In a class by itself stands the famous *Ruthwell Cross*, one of the most notable Early Christian monuments of Western Europe. Its figure sculpture, displaying strong Hellenistic influence, is of high excellence, and is accompanied by a remarkable poem in Anglian runes, in which by a highly dramatic conception the Cross is made to tell its own story of the part it played in Our Lord's Passion. According to the best judges, the Ruthwell Cross dates from the seventh century.

Apart from the sculptured stones, the monuments of the Celtic Church in Scotland are not numerous, but they include some of the first importance. Among those in the custody of the Ministry of Works are the early monastic remains on *Eileach-an-Naoimh*, in the Garvelloch Islands, showing beehive cells of Irish type; the little oratory on *Inchcolm*, which seems to have been partly refashioned in late medieval times; and the two celebrated round towers of *Abernethy* and *Brechin*. These are outliers of an Irish group, erected by the Celtic clergy as places of refuge for themselves and their holy things during the Viking invasions. The Brechin round tower is now incorporated in the thirteenth century cathedral church, but originally, like the others of its class, it stood free. Its doorway has sculpture of an Irish type. The tower can be dated to about 1000. The Abernethy round tower may be somewhat later, and its upper portion was added in Norman times.

All these are monuments of the Celtic church, as it developed during the period after the sixth century, when Scotland was cut off from the old Roman Empire by the Anglo-Saxon conquest of England. But Christianity had been introduced into Scotland when the southern half of Britain was still under Roman rule. Of this earliest mission, conducted by St. Ninian from *Whithorn* about the year 400, there still remain a notable group of monuments there and at *Kirkmadrine*. These exhibit the Chi Rho monogram, so often found on Christian monuments of the later Empire, along with Latin inscriptions commemorating persons with Roman or Romanized names. As the Celtic monastery at Whithorn was succeeded first by an Anglian bishopric and then by a Premonstratensian priory, this little place may fairly claim to have the longest continuous history of Christian worship in Britain.

THE MIDDLE AGES

THE ANGLO-NORMAN INFILTRATION

In Scotland it is usual to speak of the centuries between the Roman invasions and the Canmore dynasty as the early or Celtic period, and to restrict the terms Middle Ages, or medieval, to the period between the eleventh century and the Reformation. The distinction is a real one; for it was under the kings of the house of Canmore that Scotland was integrated into the medieval states-system as a strongly organized feudal monarchy, fashioned upon Anglo-Norman lines. In Scotland there was no Norman conquest in the English sense. We should speak rather of a Norman penetration. Under the generous patronage of the Canmore kings, from David I onwards, large numbers of Anglo-Norman settlers migrated into Galloway, Lothian, the Central Lowlands and the north-eastern plains. Sometimes by Crown grants, at other times by marrying Celtic heiresses, they obtained extensive estates. Everywhere they introduced the feudal system, and its outward and visible symbol, the feudal castle—the private stronghold of a territorial magnate exercising devolved administrative and judicial authority over his tenantry. These castles were not the ponderous stone keeps of popular imagination. Even in England such costly structures were exceptional. The ordinary Norman castle was a thing not of stone and lime but of timbered earthwork—a moated mound crowned by a palisade enclosing a wooden tower. Often there was also a banked and palisaded courtyard sheltering the household buildings, likewise in wood. We may see pictures of these structures on the Bayeux Tapestry; and they were almost the only kind of castle that existed in Scotland during the Norman penetration in the twelfth century. The Norman name for them is a *motte;* where a courtyard is attached, it is known as the *bailey*, and the entire construction may be described as a *motte* and *bailey*, or a mount and bailey castle. One of the finest in Scotland, *Duffus Castle*, near Elgin, is now under the Ministry's guardianship. It has been crowned by later stone buildings which have slipped down the Norman earthworks.

Parallel to the introduction of the Anglo-Norman baronage with their earthwork castles came the Anglo-Norman clergy bringing the Roman discipline and organization, as they had developed on the soil of the old Empire during the centuries when Celtic Scotland was largely isolated from the European states-system. Gradually the

Plate 15. *Entrance to the 'donjon', Bothwell, Lanarkshire*

Plate 16. *The east front, Elgin Cathedral, Morayshire*

Plate 17. *The chapter-house roof, Elgin Cathedral, Morayshire*

Plate 18. *Crossraguel Abbey, Ayrshire*

country was divided up into parishes, each served by a parochial priest, and the parishes were grouped into dioceses, each presided over by a bishop. So alongside the feudal castle two new items, the parish church and the cathedral, were added to the Scottish scene. In many cases the parish was just the manor of a feudal baron, ecclesiastically considered, and the parish church began as the private chapel of the lord of the manor. That is why to this day in Scotland the remains of a Norman castle are so often found close beside the parish church. Church and castle, side by side, represent respectively the ecclesiastical and the civil nuclei of the early parochial organization.

The parish priests, with their bishops, deans and other dignified superiors, were known as the secular clergy. Alongside them were introduced the regular or monastic clergy—the Benedictine and Cistercian monks, and the Augustinian canons who were a kind of intermediate clergy, living the cloistered life of monks, yet capable of undertaking a cure of souls like the parish priests. The kings of the Canmore dynasty, led by David I, were notable founders of monasteries, partly in response to the religious impulse of the time, and partly because the abbeys were civilizing agents in a wild, untutored countryside.

By the close of the thirteenth century, as a result of all these complex processes, the infeudation of at least the Scottish Lowlands had been completed. Anglo-Norman civilization was everywhere predominant, and the four chief elements in the medieval landscape—the feudal castles, the parochial churches, the cathedrals, and the abbeys—were conspicuous wherever the Norman penetration had reached. Also to the same great formative period belongs the foundation of the burghs, centres of trade and industry, established by kings, barons, or prelates, and colonized by Anglo-Norman or Flemish craftsmen and merchants. Scotland was now, comparatively speaking, a strongly organized feudal monarchy, able to resist the onslaught of Plantagenet imperialism seeking to complete the Norman conquest by force of arms, where already much of its work had been accomplished by peaceful infiltration.

CASTLES. Of the four chief elements in the medieval scene, the castles first may claim our attention. During the thirteenth century—the "Golden Age" of Alexander II and III—the earliest stone castles made their appearance in Scotland. Perhaps the oldest of these, in a typological sense, is *Castle Sween*, in Knapdale; with its great rectangular buttresses it recalls Norman construction. The finer castles of this prosperous era, such as *Dirleton*, *Hailes*, *Caerlaverock*, *Kildrummy* and *Bothwell*, are beautifully built of dressed ashlar, and have large round towers flanking curtain walls which enclose a courtyard. In these castles we may still see the destruction caused by the Scots during the struggle for independence, in accordance with Bruce's well-known policy, which was to dismantle such strongholds on their recapture from the English.

In the fourteenth century great rectangular tower-houses make their appearance, like *Threave* or *Loch Leven*. Later still these tower-houses came to be built with a wing—or "jamb", to use the Scottish term—added on one side, giving a plan like the letter L. Good examples are *Affleck Castle*, near Dundee, *Scotstarvit Tower* in Fife, and *Auchindoun* in Glenfiddich. This plan of a tower-house, whether on the simple rectangular or on the L-design, remained a favourite one among the smaller lairds until the end of the castle-building period. A late instance of its persistence is *Greenknowe Tower*, Berwickshire.

In the fourteenth and fifteenth centuries some larger castles continued to be built on the old plan of long and high curtain walls with round flanking towers. Two impressive examples are Caerlaverock and *Tantallon*. At both we can see how elaborately designed suites or lodgings came to be erected within the enclosure. Gradually it became the custom to group these symmetrically round the courtyard, and the tendency is to mass the principal apartments frontally. This process may be studied, in various forms, at the large castles of *Crichton*, *Craigmillar*, *Huntly* and *Balvenie*, and at *Linlithgow Palace*.

The introduction of firearms, and particularly of hand-guns such as could be used in the defence of a laird's house, led to the evolution of a type of castle consisting of a central mass with wings or towers echeloned at diagonally opposite corners, like the letter Z. Each tower flanks two sides of the main building, which in turn commands the towers, so that the defensive arrangement is complete. The wings or towers also supplied much additional accommodation; and, holding on as it were by their finger-tips to the central structure, they interfered as little as possible with its lighting. Excellent examples of this intriguing design are *Glenbuchat* in Strathdon, and *Claypotts* at Dundee. At *Tolquhon* we see the device adapted to a courtyard castle. Perhaps the most impressive example of the Z-plan, however, is to be found at *Noltland Castle* in the remote island of Westray, in Orkney. With its tiers of yawning gun-loops, it resembles an old man-o'-war's hulk.

Scottish castellated architecture reaches its climax about the turn of the sixteenth and seventeenth centuries. Much of the landed property of the ancient church had fallen into the hands of the lairds, and their new-found wealth expressed itself in an outburst of building. More settled internal conditions, and the end of wars with England after the

Union of the Crowns, were also circumstances favourable to architecture. To this period, accordingly, we owe such splendid pieces of early Renaissance work as Nithsdale's building at Caerlaverock, the remarkable diamonded façade at Crichton, and the upper part of Huntly Castle with its stately row of oriels. The most original design of this period is the garden wall at *Edzell Castle*, with its profuse heraldic display and its series of sculptured panels of the Planetary Deities, the Liberal Arts and the Cardinal Virtues.

CATHEDRALS. Of Scottish Cathedrals, *Glasgow*, *St. Andrews*, *Dunkeld*, *Dunblane*, *Fortrose*, *Aberdeen* (the transepts only) and *Elgin*, are in the Ministry's guardianship. The Cathedral Church of Glasgow is still complete, with the exception of two western towers, unhappily taken down in the last century. The main mass of the building is a splendid essay in the high noontide of the Gothic style, as it had developed in Britain about the year 1300. There is nothing specially Scottish about it, either in plan or in detail, since it was ordained, and mostly completed, before the War of Independence had severed Scotland's friendly relations with her southern neighbour and embarked her upon a course of intense, self-centred nationalism which would lead to the growth of a national style in her architecture. The design of the Cathedral is unique in Scotland, because it is all set out upon the central theme of St. Mungo's shrine, housed in a beautiful crypt under the presbytery. It has a broad, square-ended ambulatory round the shrine, within which the eastern end of the presbytery, likewise square, rises with a most imposing effect. According to the usual Scottish practice, the aisles are vaulted, while the nave and choir retain their fine medieval timber roofs.

The Cathedrals of St. Andrews and Elgin likewise belong in the main to the period before the War of Independence. Of St. Andrews Cathedral little save the ground plan, with the east gable, half of the west gable, and portions of the south transept have escaped destruction. About 390 feet in length, as originally designed, with a nave of fourteen bays, this was the longest church in Scotland. Beside the great Gothic cathedral stands its tiny Romanesque predecessor, the *Church of St. Rule*, or *St. Regulus*, built between 1126 and 1144. It consists of a choir, a sanctuary, and a tall square tower, west of which a nave was subsequently added. St. Rule's was built by Yorkshire masons, but the great height of its tower seems to betray Celtic influence.

The Cathedral Church of St. Mary, at Elgin, is likewise now a sorry ruin, though much more of it remains than at St. Andrews. It is unique in possessing double aisles, and the effect produced by its interior must have been one of vast spaciousness, rather than the long perspective at which medieval builders usually aimed in Britain. Strong French feeling pervades the earlier work of the church. In 1390 it was burned by the Wolf of Badenoch, being described on that melancholy occasion as "the pride of the land, the glory of the realm, the delight of wayfarers and strangers, a praise and a boast among foreign nations." To the restoration carried out in the fifteenth century belong some of the loveliest portions of the fabric, notably the vaulting of the octagonal chapter house.

The choir and presbytery of Dunkeld Cathedral have been restored and are in use as the parish church. This part of the structure retains some traces of early thirteenth century work; but the nave and west tower are a most interesting specimen of the vigorous style of two centuries later, when Scottish church architecture had taken on a strongly national cast. The plain cylindrical drums of the nave arcade, resembling those of Aberdeen Cathedral, represent a harking back to Romanesque fashion which is one of the marks of the later Scottish style. In the sanctuary is the tomb of the Wolf of Badenoch, who, notwithstanding his destruction of Elgin Cathedral, died at peace with Holy Church, and, royal ruffian as he was, was buried as beseemed a prince of the blood. The situation of Dunkeld Cathedral, on a lovely reach of the Tay, and backed by dark wooded and rocky hills, is one of great beauty. Its most famous Bishop was the poet, Gavin Douglas, the fifteenth century translator of the Aeneid, who

> *"in a barbarous age,*
> *Gave to rude Scotland Virgil's page."*

Parochial and Collegiate Churches. Of simple parish churches dating from the Middle Ages the Ministry of Works now has a number under its care up and down the country. Among these may be mentioned the churches of *Kinkell*, *Auchindoir* and *Deskford*, in the north-east, with their remarkable sacrament houses, witnesses to an artistic impulse generated by the good Bishops Elphinstone and Dunbar, and their cultured factor, Alexander Galloway, rector of Kinkell; *St. Bride's Church*, Douglas, with its fine monuments of that famous fighting race; and a remarkable group of early churches in the Orkney Islands, including the unique round church at *Orphir*—a twelfth century structure, whose remoter prototype must be sought in the Church of the Holy Sepulchre at Jerusalem. To the same period belongs the church at *Egilsay*, with a round tower built in its western gable. It is dedicated to St. Magnus, and stands on or near the site of his martyrdom.

In a class by itself stands the early sixteenth century *Church of St. Clement* at Rodel in the Isle of Harris. Cruciform in plan, with a conspicuous western tower, it is the only church of a monumental character in the outer isles. Its ornate architectural detail recalls that of Iona, and exhibits the same Irish influence and persistence of "retarded" motives. This church contains the elaborate tomb of Alastair Crottach—"the hump-backed"—eighth chief of the MacLeods of Harris and Dunvegan.

In the later Middle Ages the foundation of collegiate churches took the place of the great monasteries which had provided an outlet for the piety of an earlier generation. Such an establishment of collegiate priests was usually planted by the noble founder in the immediate neighbourhood of his residence, and a chief item in the duties of the corporation would be to celebrate mass daily for the souls of the founder and his kin. The Ministry now has five of these collegiate churches under its charge—*Maybole, Dunglass, Seton, Castle Semple* and *Lincluden.* The militarization of Scottish life, owing to the chronic war with England, had a curious result in giving these later churches a half baronial appearance. They are furnished with the battlements, crow-stepped gables, heavy vaults, and pack-saddle roofs of the feudal stronghold. This castellar effect reaches its climax in the *Preceptory Church* of the Knights Hospitallers at *Torpichen.* The least martial, and the most beautiful, of these collegiate churches is Lincluden. Its choir is a virginal piece of purest Decorated Gothic, and the tomb of the Princess Margaret Stewart, daughter of Robert III, is, perhaps, the finest thing of its kind in Scotland. Here, too, we have a well-preserved range of collegiate buildings attached to the church—the nave of which, as often in such structures, was never built.

ABBEYS. Of all the monuments in the nation's custody none are more popular than the abbeys. The rare architectural beauty of the buildings themselves, the picturesque surroundings in which most of them are situated, and the historic events and personages or literary figures with which they are connected, have combined to fix them in the public affection. Scotland is fortunate in that her four famous Border monasteries—Kelso, Melrose, Jedburgh, and Dryburgh—are all in the national keeping. In some respects the mighty ruin of *Kelso,* towering above the little town "like some antique Titan predominating over the dwarfs of a later world," is the most interesting of them all. Almost wholly in the Romanesque style, its remains are of unique importance, because the design of the church has been of Carolingian type, with transepts and a tower at both ends, east and west. *Jedburgh Abbey* is likewise mainly a Romanesque building, and, like Kelso, has a special interest for the architectural antiquary. It shows a series of heavy arches spanning the bays of the choir, arcades below the triforium, the main piers being carried right up above the latter. This arrangement is obviously an imperfect recollection of the "underslung" triforium at Oxford Cathedral. To *Melrose* belongs the literary glamour cast around its ruins by Sir Walter Scott, while the Abbey Church itself, almost wholly rebuilt after its destruction by Richard II, in 1385, is a rare and precious example of Scottish Decorated work, though the influence of English Perpendicular tracery is strongly evident on the great east window. Loveliest of all the Border abbeys, in itself and in its setting is *Dryburgh*, hallowed by the graves of Scott and Haig.

The three Cistercian abbeys of Galloway—*Dundrennan*, *Glenluce*, and *Sweetheart* or *New Abbey*—are likewise in the nation's custody. Dundrennan, a splendid ruin, saw the last that Scotland saw of the hapless Queen Mary; while the beautiful remains of Sweetheart Abbey are forever sanctified by the touching story of its origin as the abiding memorial of a great lady's love of her long dead lord. Though overshadowed by the royal palace which adjoins it, there is in all Scotland no choicer specimen of medieval church architecture than the nave of *Holyrood Abbey*. Although the building had been of no more than moderate size, its western front, with a rich portal between the towers, was one of the grandest things of its kind in Scotland. At *Arbroath Abbey* we have the imposing remains of another royal foundation, dedicated by William the Lion to the honour of St. Thomas of Canterbury. The impressive fortified gatehouse is an unusual feature, and the Abbot's House is the best example left in Scotland.

When the word "abbey" is mentioned, there naturally rises before our minds the vision of a great church. Yet it is the cloister (Latin, *claustrum*), not the church, which is the essential of the monastery; for a monk is a member of a society who by their vows are cloistered, *clausi*, or shut off from the world within the bounds of their cloister garth, so that, removed from the world's distractions, they may spend their time in prayer for the souls of the founders and benefactors of their house. It is, therefore the cloister and its buildings, rather than the church, that gives us the deepest insight into the life of a monastic community. Of the abbeys under the guardianship of the Ministry of Works, none illustrates these claustral buildings more completely than the lovely island monastery of *Inchcolm*, in the Firth of Forth. Doubtless it owes its preservation to its insular position.

THE ROYAL PALACES. In a category by themselves stand the two great national citadels of *Edinburgh* and *Stirling*, and the royal palaces of *Linlithgow* and *Holyroodhouse*. Round the castled rocks of Edinburgh and Stirling much of Scotland's turbulent history has been acted, and it is a consequence of their stormy record that the buildings in both cases are, for the most part, of comparatively modern date. At *Edinburgh* the oldest portion surviving is the little Romanesque chapel of St. Margaret. Inside the Half-moon Battery, constructed by the Regent Morton, there is still to be seen a considerable fragment of David's Tower, erected by David II between 1368 and 1379, and destroyed in the bombardment of 1573, after which the Battery was erected on top of its ruined stump. The great Hall, with its hammer-beam roof, and the Royal apartments are mostly of the sixteenth and seventeenth centuries. At *Stirling*, Cochrane's Hall, built by the unlucky favourite of James III, has been, perhaps, the finest thing of its kind in Scotland, while the royal apartments, erected by French masons, are an early and quaint example of Renaissance architecture. In James III's gatehouse and the batteries of Queen Anne's reign in front of it, we may study the difference between medieval ideas of fortification and those evolved after cannon had revolutionized the arts of attack and defence. The Chapel Royal was built by James VI for the christening of his son, Prince Henry, in 1594.

> "*Lithgow, whose palyce of plesance*
> *Micht be ane pattern in Portugall and France*";

—so wrote Sir David Lindsay of the Mount in the reign of James V; and *Linlithgow Palace* deserved all his praise, for it is without doubt the finest piece of old domestic architecture left to us in Scotland. Although built at different periods from the early fifteenth century onwards, it displays a surprising uniformity in design. Its situation, overlooking the loch, remains in all its unspoiled beauty, and the great fifteenth century town's kirk, which closely adjoins it, combines with the Palace to form a group of medieval architecture unsurpassed in the country.

The *Palace of Holyroodhouse* is indelibly associated with the tragic history of Mary Stewart, and the rooms that figured in Rizzio's murder still survive in James IV's tower; but the rest of the palace was built between 1671 and 1699 by Sir William Bruce for Charles II. A modern critic has justly observed that it "possesses a sort of refined and cultured individuality which can hardly be claimed for the great contemporary palaces of the mainland, though one of them is renowned Versailles."

NOTES

The following list of monuments in Scotland in the care of the Ministry of Works includes a brief description of each monument and information about access and admission.

Guide Books are obtainable at monuments where shown. They may also be obtained from H.M. Stationery Office—see page 2. At a number of monuments for which guide books are not yet available, the custodian has a few handboards on which the history of the building is recorded.

Postcards and in some cases colour transparencies are on sale at monuments marked with an asterisk.

Photographs may not be taken at the Palace of Holyroodhouse but may be taken elsewhere without a permit except at buildings occupied by the Military where special permission may sometimes be necessary. The use of stand cameras is subject to the discretion of the custodian.

Admission Fees. These are indicated under each monument.

Children under fourteen years of age are admitted at half price. At monuments other than Edinburgh Castle and the Palace of Holyroodhouse, parties of over twenty visitors are admitted on application to the custodian at half price. For parties of eleven to twenty in number, the fee is 5*s.* or 10*s.*

Season Tickets, price 7*s.* 6*d.* adult, 2*s.* 6*d.* child, valid for one year, admit the holder to any Monument in the Ministry's charge. They may be obtained from The Under-Secretary, Ministry of Works, 122 George Street, Edinburgh, 2.

Standard Hours of Admission are:

	Weekdays	*Sundays*
April—September ..	10 a.m.—7 p.m.	2 p.m.—7 p.m.
October—March ..	10 a.m.—4 p.m.	2 p.m.—4 p.m.

Variations from the Standard Hours are noted under the particular monument.

ABERDEENSHIRE

Brandsbutt Stone

A fine Pictish symbol stone, with a well-preserved ogham inscription. The stone was broken up to build into a field dyke, but the pieces have now been put together. Originally it formed one of a circle.

Situation. At Bransbutt, about 1 mile north-west of Inverurie.

Admission. All times without charge.

Cullerlie Stone Circle

A sepulchral stone circle of eight untrimmed boulders enclosing an area consecrated by fires on which eight small cairns were later constructed; probably of Late Bronze Age date.

Situation. Near the village of Echt, 12 miles west of Aberdeen.

Admission. All times without charge.

Culsh Earth-house

A well preserved example of an earth house with roofing slabs intact over large chamber and entrance; of Iron Age date.

Situation. At Culsh, one mile east of Tarland.

Admission. All times without charge.

**Deer Abbey*

The remains of a Cistercian monastery founded by William Comyn, Earl of Buchan, in 1218. Its predecessor, the Celtic abbey associated with the famous *Book of Deer*, was on a different site. Of the abbey church little remains, but portions of the conventual buildings stand to a fair height, and the foundations of the whole have been revealed by excavation. The church dates from the thirteenth century, but the other buildings were much reconstructed in late medieval times. The abbey is beautifully situated within a walled precinct on the banks of the River South Ugie.

Situation. Near Old Deer, 10 miles west of Peterhead.

Hours of Admission. April-September—standard. Closed in winter.

Admission. No charge.

Official Guide Pamphlet. 3*d.*

Dyce Symbol Stones

In the ruined parish church are preserved two fine examples of Pictish symbol stones. One is of the older type, with incised symbols only, while in the other the symbols are accompanied by a Celtic cross, and the sculpture is in relief and decorated with Celtic patterns.

Situation. Near Dyce, 6 miles west of Aberdeen.

Admission. All times without charge.

Glenbuchat Castle

An ancient seat of the Gordons, occupying a commanding position on upper Donside. It was built in 1590, and is a fine example of the Z-plan, having a square tower at each of two diagonally opposite corners. The stair turrets are supported, not on the usual corbelling, but by *trompes* or squinch arches in the French manner. Its last laird, John Gordon, played a notable part in the two Jacobite risings of 1715 and 1745. He escaped after Culloden and died in exile.

Situation. 14 miles west of Alford.

Admission. Not yet open to public. May be viewed from outside.

Official Guide Book for Kildrummy and Glenbuchat. 1*s.* On sale at Kildrummy.

★Huntly Castle

One of the noblest baronial ruins in Scotland, this castle, formerly known as Strathbogie Castle, was the headquarters of the "gay Gordons". In the 16th and 17th centuries its rulers, the Earls and Marquises of Huntly, were the most powerful magnates in the north, and leaders of the Catholic cause in the Counter-reformation struggle. Hence this castle was much involved in the religious wars of that time, and repeatedly underwent dismantling and reconstruction. The site is a Norman one, and is still marked by the earthworks of a large mount and bailey. On the east side is a ravelin dating from the Civil War. The remains of the stone castle comprise the foundations of a strong 15th century tower-house, destroyed in 1594, and an imposing hall-house or "palace", with a great round tower and a smaller one containing the stair. The heraldic enrichments of this building are the most elaborate in Scotland, and its row of oriels are a reminiscence of Blois. The castle stands in a beautifully timbered park beside the rocky gorge of the Deveron, here spanned by an ancient bridge.

Situation. In Huntly.

Hours of Admission. Standard.

Admission Fee. 6*d.*

Official Guide Book. 1*s.*

**Kildrummy Castle* (Plate 13.)

"The noblest of northern castles", and the most complete example in Scotland of a secular building dating from the 13th century. The wall of *enceinte*, with four round towers, in greater or lesser preservation, the hall, and the chapel with its fine three-light window, belong in substance to the original fabric. The great gatehouse is Edwardian, and there is later work of the 15th and 16th centuries. The barbican with its drawbridge pit is of considerable interest. This castle was the seat of the Earls of Mar, and played a memorable part in Scottish history from the Wars of Independence until the "Fifteen", when it was dismantled.

Situation. On the Don, 10 miles west of Alford.

Admission. All times without charge.

Official Guide Book for Kildrummy and Glenbuchat. 1*s.*

Kinkell Church

The ruins of an early sixteenth century parish church, with some ornate details, including a rich sacrament house of unusual design, dated 1524. In the church is the monument of Gilbert de Greenlaw, slain at the battle of Harlaw (1411).

Situation. On the Don, 2 miles south of Inverurie.

Admission. All times without charge.

Loanhead Stone Circle

The best known example of a widespread group of recumbent stone circles in east Scotland; the circle enclosed a kerbed ring cairn built over the site of a cremation pyre; dates to the transitional period Neolithic-Bronze Age (*c.* 1800 B.C.) but was in use at a later date.

Situation. Near the hamlet of Daviot, 5 miles north-north-west of Inverurie.

Admission. All times without charge.

Maiden Stone (Plate 10.)

The most famous of the Early Christian monuments in Aberdeenshire, this stone is associated with several weird legends formerly current in the Garioch. On one side it displays a richly ornamented Celtic cross and other decoration in the same style, and on the other side are Pictish symbols.

Situation. Near Chapel of Garioch, 4½ miles north-west of Inverurie (by Drumdurno Farm).

Admission. All times without charge.

Memsie Burial Cairn

A fine example of a large stone-built cairn probably dating to the Bronze Age (*c.* 1500 B.C.).

Situation. Near the village of Rathen, 3½ miles south of Fraserburgh.

Admission. All times without charge.

Peel Ring of Lumphanan

Major early medieval earthwork, consisting of a large oval motte or mound defended by a wet ditch. Masonry foundations can be traced on the summit. Lumphanan is said to have been the scene of Macbeth's final defeat in 1057, and was visited by Edward I of England in 1296.

Situation. Half a mile south-west of Lumphanan and 22 miles west of Aberdeen (Route A. 980). Infrequent bus service from Aberdeen.

Admission. All times without charge.

Picardy Stone

A Pictish symbol stone of the oldest class, with incised symbols.

Situation. Near Mireton, Insch.

Admission. All times without charge.

St. Machar's Cathedral, Aberdeen

Only the nave, western towers, and transepts of this cathedral now remain. The nave is in use as a parish church, but the transepts are ruined and under the guardianship of the Ministry. The two west piers of the crossing date from *circa* 1380 and show figure sculpture and "knife-cut" foliage, closely resembling contemporary work at Melrose. In the south transept is the fine altar tomb of Bishop Dunbar (1514-32).

Situation. In Old Aberdeen.

Admission. All times without charge.

St. Mary's Church, Auchindoir

One of the finest medieval parish churches remaining in Scotland: roofless but otherwise entire. It has a rich Norman-Transitional doorway, some good First Pointed details, and a beautiful early sixteenth century sacrament house (*cf.* Deskford, Kinkell). There are also some interesting sixteenth century heraldic monuments.

Situation. Near to village of Lumsden, 3 miles north of Kildrummy.

Admission. All times without charge.

Tarves Medieval Tomb

A fine altar-tomb of William Forbes, the laird who enlarged Tolquhon Castle. It shows an interesting commixture of Gothic and Renaissance styles.

Situation. In the kirkyard of Tarves, 15 miles north-north-west of Aberdeen.

Admission. All times without charge.

**Tolquhon Castle*

A seat of the Forbes family. Its nucleus is a strong rectangular tower, dating from the early fifteenth century. To this was added, between 1584 and 1589, a large quadrangular mansion, now roofless but otherwise in a very complete state of preservation. This mansion admirably illustrates the great advance in domestic planning during the reign of James VI. A notable feature is the gatehouse with its two round towers, armorial bearings, and quaint figure sculpture. The castle is remarkable for the variety of its ornate gun-loops. There is a large forecourt with outbuildings, and a spacious pleasance, still graced by rows of venerable yews and hollies.

Situation. 15 miles from Aberdeen off the Pitmedden-Tarves Road.

Hours of Admission. Standard.

Admission Fee. 6*d.*

Official Guide Pamphlet. 3*d.*

Tomnaverie Stone Circle

The remains of a recumbent stone circle probably of Bronze Age date. Unexcavated.

Situation. Near Mill of Wester Coull, about 3 miles north-west of Aboyne.

Admission. All times without charge.

ANGUS

Aberlemno Sculptured Stones

Consisting of a splendid upright cross-slab, with Pictish symbols and figure sculpture on the reverse, in Aberlemno kirkyard, and three stones at the farm of Flemington, one of which bears incised symbols and another a cross and dragonesque creatures in front, and symbols and figure sculpture on the reverse.

Situation. At Aberlemno, 6 miles north-east of Forfar.

Admission. All times without charge.

**Affleck Castle*

A late fifteenth century tower-house on the L-plan, still in perfect condition. Four storeys in height, turretted and battlemented, it is noteworthy for the elaborate and advanced character of its internal arrangements. Off the solar, or upper hall, there is a very beautiful little chapel, or oratory, and the solar itself is a room of exceptional distinction, which, despite its small size, has few equals in Scotland. The castle was the residence of the ancient family of Auchinleck or Affleck of that ilk.

Situation. At Monikie, 9 miles north-east of Dundee.

Admission. All reasonable times, except Sundays, on application to custodian.

Admission Fee. 6*d.*

Official Guide Pamphlet. 2*d.*

★*Arbroath Abbey*

The imposing remains of a Tironensian monastery founded in 1176 by William the Lion. It was dedicated to St. Thomas of Canterbury. Here in 1320 a great assembly of the nation issued the famous Declaration of Arbroath, in which, in words of deathless pride, they asserted Scottish independence against the encroachments of Plantagenet England. Considerable portions of the cruciform abbey church remain, including an aiseless presbytery, transeptal chapels and two western towers. The best preserved portion is the south transept, with its rose window. The great west doorway had above it a tribune, like those at Holyrood and St. Andrews. Important remains of the claustral buildings also survive, including the "pend" or vaulted entrance, the embattled "regality tower" and the abbot's house, which has been restored as a museum.

Situation. In Arbroath.

Hours of Admission. Standard.

Admission Fee. 1*s.*

Official Guide Book. 1*s.* 6*d.* The Guide Book to Early Christian & Pictish Monuments of Scotland is also available. Price 5*s.*

Ardestie and Carlungie Earth-houses

Two examples of large earthhouses attached to surface dwellings. At Ardestie the gallery is curved and 80 feet in length; the Carlungie souterrain is 150 feet long and is most complex; occupied in first centuries A.D.

Situation. About 7 miles east of Dundee.

Admission. All times without charge.

Brechin: Maison Dieu Chapel

This is an interesting fragment of mid-thirteenth century ecclesiastical architecture. The ruins consist of a portion of the south wall of the chapel and a small extent of the east wall. The details of the doors and windows are unusually fine. The chapel is said to have been founded in 1256 by William de Brechin. The structure, as the name implies, doubtless formed part of a hospital.

Situation. In the centre of the town of Brechin.

Admission. All reasonable times, on application to custodian.

Brechin: Round Tower

One of the two remaining round towers of the Irish type in Scotland (see also ABERNETHY, PERTHSHIRE). It dates from about 1000 and is now attached to the thirteenth century cathedral. The doorway with its figure sculpture is of characteristic Irish design. The spire is an addition of the fourteenth century

Situation. In Brechin.

Admission. Can be closely viewed from the churchyard.

Broughty Castle

A large oblong structure with a battlemented top: erected about the beginning of the sixteenth century.

Situation. In Broughty Ferry.

Admission. All reasonable times without charge. Administered by Dundee Corporation.

The Caterthuns:

Situation. Near the village of Menmuir, about 5 miles north-west of Brechin.

Admission. All times without charge.

The Brown Caterthun

An excellent example of an Iron Age hill fort with four concentric ramparts and ditches interrupted by entrances and causeways; unexcavated.

The White Caterthun

A well-preserved hill fort of Iron Age date (*c.* 200 B.C.) with massive stone rampart and defensive ditch and outer earthworks.

★*Claypotts* (Plate 23.)

This singular edifice bears the dates 1569 and 1588, and was a seat of the Strachan family. Later it belonged to the celebrated John Graham of Claverhouse, Viscount Dundee. It is still entire, roof and all, and is a valuable specimen of a fortified residence on the "three-stepped" or Z-plan, having a round tower at each of two diagonally opposite corners. These towers are corbelled out to form overhanging cap-houses in a remarkably picturesque manner. The ground floor of the castle is well provided with wide-mouthed gun-loops.

Situation. Broughty Ferry.

Hours of Admission. Standard.

Admission Fee. 6*d.*

Official Guide Book. 1*s.*

Eassie Sculptured Stone

A fine example of the elaborately sculptured Early Christian monuments of Angus. On the front is a richly decorated Celtic cross, with figure and animal subjects, and on the back are Pictish symbols and processional scenes.

Situation. In the old churchyard of Eassie: on the Glamis-Meigle road.

Admission. All times without charge.

★*Edzell Castle*

This, the ancient seat of the Lindsays of Glenesk, was the most splendid castle in Angus. The oldest part is a fine tower-house, dating from the early sixteenth century. To this a quadrangular mansion was added by the ninth Earl of Crawford later in that century; and in 1602 the buildings were completed by his son, Sir David Lindsay, Lord Edzell, who added a spacious walled garden or pleasance, with a bath-house and summer-house. The garden wall exhibits a display of heraldic and symbolical decoration unique in Britain, including a series of sculptured panels portraying the Cardinal Virtues, the Liberal Arts, and the Planetary Deities. These subjects have been shown to be of German inspiration.

Situation. At Edzell, 6 miles north of Brechin.

Hours of Admission. Standard.

Admission Fee. 1*s.*

Official Guide Book. 1*s.*

Restenneth Priory

A house of Augustinian canons regular, probably founded by David I. It was burned by Edward I, but recovered its prosperity under the patronage of Robert Bruce, a son of whom, Prince Robert, is buried here. The most prominent feature of the ruins is the tall square tower, with its shapely broach spire. The lower part of the tower exhibits very early Romanesque work, the date of which has been much argued. There is a fine thirteenth century chancel, but of the nave and claustral buildings little or nothing remains. The surroundings of the priory are very beautiful.

Situatuon. 1½ miles east of Forfar.

Hours of Admission. Standard.

Admission Fee. 6d.

Official Guide Pamphlet. 3*d.*

St. Orland's Stone

An upstanding sculptured slab of the Early Christian period: on one side a cross in relief extending from the top to bottom; on either side of the cross shaft and upon the shaft and arms a variety of interlaced patterns executed in low relief. On the other side an assemblage of figure subjects; men on horseback depicting a hunting scene; men in a boat; two animals; the crescent and V-rod symbol, and the double disc and Z-rod symbol.

Situation. In a field near the farmhouse of Cossans 1½1miles north-east of Glamis railway station: 4½ miles west of Forfar.

Admission. All times without charge.

Tealing Dovecot

A good example of a late sixteenth century dovecot.

Tealing Earth-house

A well-preserved example of a souterrain or earth-house comprising a passage and long curved gallery and small inner chamber; of Iron Age date.

Situation. 5 miles north of Dundee.

Admission. All times without charge.

ARGYLL

Achnabreck

The exposed crest of a rocky ridge covered with well-preserved cup-and-ring scribings of Bronze Age date.

Situation. 1½ miles north-west of Lochgilphead.

Admission. All times without charge.

Ardchattan Priory

One of the three Valliscaulian houses founded in Scotland in 1230 (see under Beauly, infra. p. 93). The remains are much mixed up with a modern mansion house, but include some vigorous First Pointed work, also several monuments in the characteristic late West-Highland style. The priory was burned by Cromwell's soldiery in 1654.

Situation. On north side of Loch Etive, 6½ miles N.E. of Oban.

Admission. All times without charge.

Ballygowan

Cup-and-ring scribings on natural rock faces; dating to the Bronze Age.

Situation. 1 mile south-west of Kilmartin, near Poltalloch.

Admission. All times without charge.

Baluachraig

Several groups of Bronze Age cup-and-ring scribings on natural rock faces.

Situation. 1 mile south-south-east of Kilmartin.

Admission. All times without charge.

Cairnbaan

A group of Bronze Age cup-and-ring scribings on a natural rock surface.

Situation. 200 yards north-west of the Cairnbaan Hotel, 2½ miles N.W. of Lochgilphead.

Admission. All times without charge.

Carnasserie Castle

This very attractive castle was the house of John Carswell, first Protestant Bishop of the Isles, who translated Knox's *Liturgy* into Gaelic, and published it in 1567. It was the first book printed in that language. The castle was captured and partly blown up during Argyll's rebellion in 1685. It consists of a tower-house with a hall-house attached, but the whole building is of one date and design. Its architectural details are unusually fine for a West Highland castle.

Situation. 2 miles N. of Kilmartin.

Admission. All times without charge.

Castle Sween

This lonely ruin, situated on the rocky western coast of Knapdale, is of high architectural importance, since it appears to be, typologically considered, the earliest stone castle in Scotland. It was probably built in the mid twelfth century, and the main structure is quite of a Norman aspect, with large pilaster and angle buttresses. A great oblong tower-house, with pointed loopholes, and a cylindrical angle tower, are later additions. The castle was destroyed by Sir Alexander Macdonald in 1647.

Situation. On the east shore of Loch Sween, in South Knapdale.

Admission. All times without charge.

Plate 19. *West Highland grave slabs, Kilmory Knap, Argyll*

Plate 20. *Detail from West Highland grave slab, Kilmartin, Argyll*

Plate 19. *West Highland grave slabs, Kilmory Knap, Argyll*

Plate 20. *Detail from West Highland grave slab, Kilmartin, Argyll*

Plate 21. *Macmillan's Cross, Kilmory Knap, Argyll*

Plate 22. *Hermitage Castle, Roxburghshire*

Plate 23. *Claypotts, Angus*

Plate 24. *Tempera decoration, Kinneil House, West Lothian*

Dunadd Fort

A well-preserved Dark Age hill-fort with walled enclosures, identified as the capital of Dalriada, the primitive Kingdom of the Scots.

Situation. 1 mile west of Kilmichael Glassary.

Admission. All times without charge.

Dunchraigaig

A denuded Bronzed Age cairn; originally covered three burial cists containing inhumed and cremated human bones.

Situation. 1¼ miles south of Kilmartin.

Admission. All times without charge.

Dunstaffnage Castle

An exceptionally fine and well preserved example of a thirteenth century castle of *enceinte*, built on a rock, and showing the usual great curtain wall and round towers. Close beside it is a ruined chapel in a very rich First Pointed style, showing exceptional refinement and beauty in its architectural detail. The castle has a long and colourful history extending from the War of Independence to the Forty Five. Traditionally Dunstaffnage is the site of an early seat of the Dalriadic Kings, and it is said that the Stone of Destiny was kept there before its removal to Scone.

Situation. On the shore of Loch Etive, 3½ miles north of Oban.

Admission. Work in progress: free admission during working hours.

Eileach-an-Naoimh

An island with a most interesting group of Celtic monastic remains. It is intimately associated in local tradition with St. Columba, and may be the *Hinba* of Adamnan. The remains include beehive cells, a chapel, and a graveyard.

Situation. One of the Garvelloch Isles, in the Firth of Lorne.

Admission. All times without charge; by hired motor boat from Cullipool or Easdale. Telephone:

Eilean Mor: St. Cormac's Chapel

This chapel consists of nave and chancel, the latter vaulted, and entered by a round arch. It contains the effigy of an ecclesiastic.

Situation. On an islet off the coast of Knapdale.

Admission. All times without charge; access is difficult; by privately hired motor-boat, from Crinan Hotel.

Inchkenneth Chapel

A unicameral chapel of the West Highland type, with pointed windows. The burial ground contains several interesting medieval monuments, including the figure of a mailed warrior.

Situation. On the Island of Inchkenneth, in Loch-na-Keal, on the west side of Mull.

Admission. All reasonable times without charge on application to custodian, Mr. I. Cochrane, Gribun, Mull; by hired motor-boat.

Iona: Maclean's Cross

A fine fifteenth century free-standing cross of the Hebridean type, on the road from the village to the Cathedral. It displays a Crucifixion and foliaceous interlaced work. The cross is said to commemorate a Maclean of Duart.

Situation. On the island of Iona.

Admission. All times without charge.

Kilberry Sculptured Stones

A collection of late medieval sculptured stones from the Kilberry estate.

Situation. Kilberry Castle, 17 miles S.S.W. of Lochgilphead on the west coast of Knapdale.

Admission. All times without charge.

Kilchurn Castle

This castle dates from the middle of the fifteenth century when it was built by Sir Colin Campbell of Glenorchy, the founder of the Breadalbane family. It stands prominently in a marsh at the end of Loch Awe, in a situation of great natural beauty. The oldest part of the castle is a high, square tower. The additional buildings, erected in 1693, converted this once free-standing tower into a castle surrounding an irregular courtyard.

Situation. At the north-east end of Loch Awe, 2½ miles west of Dalmally; clearly visible from the main road.

Admission. All times without charge.

Kilmartin: Churchyard Crosses (Plate 20.)

In this typical West Highland churchyard are preserved a collection of grave slabs and fragments of at least two crosses, one showing Christ crucified on the obverse and Christ in Majesty on the reverse. The former figure is carved with exceptional refinement and feeling. Although the cross dates from the sixteenth century, the influence of twelfth century ivory work is clearly seen in the Christ in Majesty.

Situation. In Kilmartin.

Admission. All times without charge.

Kilmartin: Glebe Cairn

When excavated in 1864 the cairn, built entirely of stones, was found to contain two cists. One cist was lined with boulders and covered by a slab; the second was made entirely of slabs. This latter contained a beaker and a necklace of jet beads. Of Early Bronze Age date (*c.* 1800 B.C.).

Situation. Kilmartin Glebe.

Admission. All times without charge.

Kilmichael Glassary

Cup-and-ring scribings of Bronze Age date on natural rock outcrop.

Situation. Near schoolhouse.

Admission. All times without charge.

Kilmory Knap: Chapel (Plate 19 & 21.)

A typical small church of the West Highlands, unicameral and with a pair of round arched east windows. There is an assemblage of late medieval sculptured stones in the chapel and in the kirkyard Macmillan's Cross.

Situation. In south Knapdale, on the shore between Loch Sween and Loch Caolisport.

Admission. All times without charge.

Nether Largie Cairns:

Situation. Between Kilmartin and Nether Largie.

Admission. All times without charge. Key for the North Cairn at Kilmartine Hotel.

North Cairn

The northernmost of three cairns erected at the side of an ancient trackway and covering a central burial cist with large capstone bearing cup marks and representations of flat copper axe heads; of Bronze Age date (*c.* 1500 B.C.).

Mid Cairn

A despoiled cairn, one of a line of three built at the side of an ancient trackway, and originally containing two burial cists constructed of stone slabs, grooved and adorned with cup-and-ring marks; of Early Bronze Age date (*c.* 1800-1500 B.C.).

South Cairn

A fine example of a megalithic chambered cairn of the Clyde type with segmented cist. The long narrow cist is well preserved, dating back to the Neolithic or Late Stone Age (*c.* 2000 B.C.).

Ri Cruin Cairn

A despoiled burial cairn of Bronze Age date originally covering three stone cists. Axe figures are engraved on one of the cist slabs.

Situation. 1 mile south-west of Kilmartin.

Admission. All times without charge.

Temple Wood Stone Circle

A circle of upright stones, now much reduced in number, with a burial cist at the centre; probably of Bronze Age date (*c.* 1500 B.C.).

Situation. ¼ mile south-west of Nether Largie.

Admission. All times without charge.

AYRSHIRE

**Crossraguel Abbey* (Plate 18.)

A Cluniac monastery founded by Duncan, Earl of Carrick, in 1244, as a subordinate house of Paisley. It was much patronized by the Bruces, and by the early Stewart monarchs. A famous event in its history is the roasting of Abbot Stewart, in 1570, by the Earl of Cassillis, with the object of forcing him to surrender his title deeds. The remains of the abbey are very extensive and of high architectural distinction. They consist of the church, claustral buildings, outer court with an imposing castellated gatehouse, and abbot's house with a strong tower attached. The choir of the church, with its three-sided apse, is a fine specimen of the latest phase in Scottish Gothic, and the sacristy and chapter-house, of the same late date, are likewise very rich.

Situation. 2 miles from Maybole on the main Maybole-Girvan road.

Hours of Admission. Standard.

Admission Fee. 1*s.*

Card Guide. 2*d.*

Dundonald Castle

King Robert II, the first Stuart King, rebuilt this castle, which became his favourite residence. He died here in 1390. The king's chief work at Dundonald consists of a very large oblong tower-house, remarkable in itself and for the way in which it incorporates the remains of a 13th century gatehouse. Most of this tower, and much of the barmkin wall survive. The castle stands on an isolated hill and is a notable landmark.

Situation. About midway between Kilmarnock and Irvine; on Kilmarnock-Irvine road.

Admission. Not yet open to the public. May be closely viewed from the outside.

Loch Doon Castle

This castle now stands upon the shores of Loch Doon where it was transplanted some years ago from its original site in the middle of the loch on the consequence of the raising of the water level. The earliest records of the castle date it to the early fourteenth century. Its plan is unusual. The castle consists of a great curtain wall of eleven unequal sides. The walls vary in thickness from 7 feet to 9 feet and stand about 26 feet high. The masonry is of the most excellent kind. The main entrance consists of a fine pointed doorway of late thirteenth century or early fourteenth century character. It was defended by a portcullis.

Situation. 10 miles south of Dalmellington.

Admission. All times without charge.

Maybole Collegiate Church

The roofless ruin of a fifteenth century church, built for a small college established here in 1373 by the Kennedies of Dunure. The remains include a rich door in a revived First Pointed style, and an Easter Sepulchre which is also an imitation of early work. In the provost's house, now gone, John Knox had his famous disputation with Quentin Kennedy in 1561.

Situation. In Maybole.

Admission. Not yet open to the public, visible from the street.

Rowallan Castle

This house is a fine specimen of a superior Scottish mansion of the sixteenth and seventeenth centuries. It is distinguished architecturally by two imposing round towers with conical roofs which flank the entrance at first floor level.

The outer entrance to the castle forecourt is through a fine sculptured doorway in the Renaissance style. The castle has a very pleasant situation in a well-timbered park on the banks of the Carmel stream.

Situation. About 3 miles north of Kilmarnock.

Admission. Not open to the public meantime. May be viewed from outside.

★Skelmorlie Aisle, Largs

A splendid example of a Renaissance monument: erected by Sir Robert Montgomery of Skelmorlie in 1636. The monument stands in an aisle, formerly the north transept of the old church of Largs, and is the only portion now preserved. The roof of the aisle is a timber barrel-vault divided into compartments with painted ribs imitating a rib-vaulted roof. Within the panels are painted scenes representing the old castle of Skelmorlie, Largs Church, emblematical subjects, signs of the Zodiac and heraldic devices. The monument, which is built in stone, consists of a gallery raised above a partially sunk burial vault. The gallery is reached by a short stair. It is surmounted by an elaborate architectural devisement of Corinthian columns and classical entablatures supporting as a central feature a coffered barrel-vault crowned with foliated and interlaced scroll-work mingled with cupids, hour glasses, obelisks, etc. The whole effect is extremely rich.
Another monument in the same art style, though greatly inferior, is built against the south wall on the outside, to the memory of the Boyles of Kelburn. The exuberant classicism of the Montgomery monument makes it one of the most remarkable examples of its type and period in Scotland.

Situation. In Largs.

Admission. April-September, 10 a.m. to 5.30 p.m.

Admission Fee. 6d.

BANFFSHIRE

Auchindoun Castle

A massive ruin grandly situated on the summit of an isolated hill, enclosed by prehistoric earthworks. The central tower was built by the master mason, Thomas Cochran, the ill-starred favourite of James III. It had a groin-vaulted hall, the ribs of which were wrongly set out, so that a new start had to be made, but the difficulty was overcome in a most effective and picturesque manner. In Queen Mary's wars this was the stronghold of the redoubtable "Edom o' Gordon". The courtyard buildings were probably erected by him. Here the Jacobite leaders held a council of war after Dundee's death at Killiecrankie.

Situation. In Glen Fiddich, 2½ miles south-east of Dufftown.

Admission. All times without charge.

★Balvenie Castle

This ancient stronghold of the Comyns, visited by Edward I in 1304, belonged subsequently to the Black Douglases and the Stewart Earls of Atholl, and was visited by Queen Mary in 1562. It had a disturbed history during the wars of the seventeenth century, and was occupied by the Hanoverians in 1746. Its great enclosing curtain wall, girt by a rock-hewn ditch, is a work of the Comyn period, but most of the existing buildings were erected in the fifteenth and sixteenth centuries. This is one of the largest and best preserved castles in the north of Scotland. A remarkable feature is the two-leaved iron yett.

Situation. At Dufftown.

Hours of Admission. Standard.

Admission Fee. 6*d.*

Official Guide Pamphlet. 2*d.*

Deskford Church

This ruined building possesses a rich sacrament house, of the type peculiar to the north-east of Scotland during the early sixteenth century (*c.f.* Kinkell). It bears an inscription telling that "this present lovable work of sacrament house" was provided by Alexander Ogilvy of Deskford in 1551.

Situation. 4 miles south of Cullen.

Admission. All times without charge.

BERWICKSHIRE

**Dryburgh Abbey*

One of the famous group of Border monasteries founded in the reign of David I. It was a house of Premonstratensian canons, and the founder was Hugh de Morville, Constable of Scotland. The ruins, in themselves of extreme beauty, occupy a lovely situation in a horseshoe bend of the Tweed, and are of high architectural interest because, though little save the transepts has been spared of the church itself, the claustral buildings have survived in a more complete state than in any other Scottish monastery, except Iona and Inchcolm. A great deal of the existing remains, moreover, dates from the twelfth and thirteenth centuries, though there has also been much reconstruction following on the burning of the abbey by Richard II in 1385. Both the early and the later work are marked by extreme refinement. Within the church are the graves of Sir Walter Scott and Earl Haig.

Situation. 5 miles south-east of Melrose, near St. Boswells.

Hours of Admission. Standard.

Admission Fee. 1*s.*

Official Guide Book. 1*s.* 6*d.*

Edin's Hall Broch

Listed among the five Iron Age brochs known in Lowland Scotland. Its dimensions are exceptionally large; the structure was originally defended by a series of outworks.

Situation. On the north-eastern slope of Cockburn Law, about 4½ miles from Grantshouse, by the Duns Road.

Admission. All times without charge.

Edrom Church

Of the ancient and now ruined Parish Church of Edrom, there survives a Norman doorway of great beauty. Its survival is due to its incorporation and use in a burial vault erected against it. The doorway consists of a round arched opening in three orders, with angle shafts. The capitals of the shafts and the three orders of the arch are richly carved with Norman decorative details.

Situation. In Edrom. 3½ miles north-east of Duns.

Admission. All times without charge.

Foulden Tithe Barn

A two-storeyed tithe barn in two floors; outside stair and crow-stepped gables. Complete.

Situation. Foulden, 4 miles south-east of Chirnside, on the Chirnside-Berwick road.

Admission. Not open to the public; may be closely viewed from the roadside.

Greenknowe Tower

A fine turreted tower-house on the L-plan, dated 1581, and still retaining its iron yett. Built by James Seton of Touch, whose armorial bearings it displays, it became in the next century the seat of Walter Pringle, the noted Covenanter.

Situation. 1 mile west of Gordon, on the Duns-Earlston road.

Admission. All reasonable times without charge, on application to custodian.

BUTE

Auchagallon Stone Circle

A Bronze Age burial cairn surrounded by a circle of fifteen standing stones.

Situation. By the east side of a farm road 4 miles north of Blackwaterfoot.

Admission. All times without charge.

Lochranza Castle

Substantial remains of what is probably a sixteenth century building sited at the extremity of a peninsula jutting out into the loch. The existence of a castle on this site is first recorded at the end of the fourteenth century.

Situation. Lochranza, Arran. Access by Clyde Coast steamer.

Admission. Free on application to key-keeper, Mr. T. Kerr, Post Office, Lochranza.

**Rothesay Castle*

This is one of the most remarkable and important medieval castles in Scotland. It dates from the early thirteenth century and is an outstanding example of the typical thirteenth century castle distinguished by high curtain walls fortified by projecting drum towers. The curtain walls stand to a height of some 30 feet. The castle differs from the normal plan in that the walls enclose a circular courtyard. This plan form is unique in Scotland. The site is surrounded by a deep water moat. The entrance way is through a high tower which projects boldly into the moat. This fore-tower is the work of James IV and James V. Within the courtyard may be seen the foundations of sundry internal buildings, haphazardly disposed, and the roofless shell of a chapel. In all probability the castle may represent in substance that captured by the Norsemen in the year 1230.

Situation. In the centre of Rothesay, Isle of Bute.

Hours of Admission. Standard.

Admission Fee. 1*s.*

Official Guide Pamphlet. 3*d.*

St. Mary's Chapel, Rothesay

Late medieval remains of the Abbey Church of St. Mary, originally the chancel, including two fine recessed and canopied tombs containing effigies of a knight in full armour, and a lady and child.

Situation. Rothesay, Bute.

Admission. Free on application to custodian at Rothesay Castle.

CAITHNESS

Castle of Old Wick

A ruined square tower of four unvaulted storeys, standing on a spine of rock projecting into the sea, between two deep narrow gulleys or geos, about one mile south of Wick. It belonged to the Cheynes, later to the Sutherlands of Duffus, and was besieged and taken by the Master of Caithness in 1569. The tower probably dates from the fourteenth century.

Situation. 1 mile south of Wick.

Admission. All times without charge.

Grey Cairns of Camster

Two megalithic chambered cairns of Neolithic date (*c.* 2000 B.C.). One cairn is elongated with expanded ends or "horns" and contains two chambers. The other is round and contains a single chamber approached by a passage which is at present blocked.

Situation. 5 miles north of Lybster, on the west side of the Lybster-Watten road.

Admission. At all times without charge.

St. Mary's Chapel, Crosskirk

A rudely-constructed chapel consisting of chancel and nave, access from one to the other being by a low and narrow doorway with inclining jambs: probably of twelfth century date. At the cliff edge nearby are the remains of a broch.

Situation. Crosskirk, on the coast, 6 miles west of Thurso.

Admission. All times without charge.

CLACKMANNANSHIRE

★Castle Campbell

The castle consists of a lofty oblong tower erected in the third quarter of the fifteenth century, and later buildings added in the sixteenth and seventeenth centuries. The castle is situated on the top of a rocky mound rising precipitously from the deep ravines of the beautiful Dollar Glen. From the castle a magnificent panorama over the Forth and the plains beyond is no less picturesque. The early tower is in a very good state of preservation and contains a fine stone vaulted ceiling. Fronting the courtyard in one of the later ranges is an unusual loggia of sixteenth century date. Such external corridors are uncommon in Scotland but at Falkland Palace there is a somewhat similar feature and there is evidence of another in St. Andrews Castle.

Situation. At the head of Dollar Glen, Dollar.

Hours of Admission. Standard.

Admission Fee. 6*d.*

Official Guide Book. 1*s.*

Telephone No.: Dollar 208.

Clackmannan Tower

This interesting castle stands on a commanding site overlooking the town of Clackmannan. Before its partial collapse due to subsidence it was one of the most complete and complicated of Scottish tower-houses. It began as a fourteenth century tower, to which a "jamb" or wing was added in the next century and it is now a tall and martial edifice, embattled and turreted. From 1365 until 1772 the castle belonged to the Bruce family. It was formerly surrounded by a moat.

Situation. In Clackmannan.

Admission. No facilities for entry whilst work is in progress: may be closely viewed from the outside.

DUMFRIESSHIRE

★*Caerlaverock Castle*

The chief seat of the Maxwell family, and one of the foremost examples of medieval secular architecture in Scotland. It is famous in history and literature through its siege by Edward I in 1300, commemorated in the well-known old French poem, *Le Siège de Karlaverok.* In 1640 it was captured by the Covenanters and dismantled. The ruins, which stand within a wide moat, include much work of the thirteenth and fifteenth centuries; and the latest building, dating from 1638, is one of the finest examples of early classical Renaissance in Scotland. The shape of the castle is very remarkable, being triangular, like a shield, with a round tower at each of the two basal angles and a great gatehouse at the apex.

Situation. About 8 miles south-south-east of Dumfries.

Access. Bus service from Dumfries to Glencaple; thence three miles' walk.

Hours of Admission. Standard.

Admission Fee. 6*d.*

Official Guide Book. 1*s.*

Kirkconnel Churchyard

Within this ancient burial place are the foundations of the Norman church of St. Connel, and a number of carved fragments, including portions of

Anglian crosses, may be seen in the kirkyard dyke: but the main interest of the place centres on the gravestone of "Fair Helen of Kirkconnel Lea," and her lover, Adam Fleming, whose tragic fate forms the theme of one of the sweetest of Scottish ballads.

Situation. In Annandale, near Kirtlebridge.

Admission. All times without charge.

**Lincluden College*

In 1164 a Benedictine nunnery was founded here by Uchtred, Lord of Galloway. At the end of the fourteenth century this was suppressed by Archibald the Grim, third Earl of Douglas, who established in its place a college of eight secular canons under a provost. The existing remains are those of the collegiate church and the provost's house. The church, of which the chancel and south aisle and transept survive, dates from the early fifteenth century, and is one of the most beautiful pieces of Decorated architecture left to us in Scotland. It is remarkable for the richness of its heraldic adornment, for the noble tomb of the Princess Margaret, daughter of Robert III, and for the *pulpitum* or carved stone screen separating the chancel from the nave. The provost's house dates from the sixteenth century. Adjoining the church is a Norman *motte*, later terraced as part of a pleasance.

Situation. On the western outskirts of Dumfries.

Hours of Admission. Standard.

Admission Fee. *6d.*

Lochmaben Castle

The extensive ruin, yet fragmentary and hard to interpret, of the famous castle of the Bruces, stands on a promontory jutting into the loch of the same name, and isolated by strong earthworks and an ashlar-lined moat. Its history is complicated by the existence, close to Lochmaben town, of a large *motte*, which no doubt was the earlier castle, famous in the Wars of Independence, and destroyed finally by the Scots in 1384. The existing castle seems to have been mainly built in the reign of James IV. During Lord Maxwell's Catholic rising in 1588, the castle was bombarded and captured by James VI, and was allowed to fall into decay in the next century.

Situation. On the shore of Lochmaben.

Admission. Work in progress; free admission during working hours.

Merkland Cross

A fine fifteenth century floriated wayside cross, concerning which various legends are current locally.

Situation. At Merkland Smithy, in Kirkpatrick-Fleming parish, near Ecclefechan.

Admission. All times without charge.

Ruthwell Cross

Preserved in an annexe to the parish church, this ranks, along with the Bewcastle Cross in Cumberland, as one of the two foremost examples of Anglian sculpture, and is one of the major monuments of Dark Age Europe. The cross, which has been slightly restored, dates probably from the end of the seventh century. The main faces have figure-sculpture, mostly scriptural scenes, associated with Latin inscriptions, and on the sides are rich vine scrolls with birds and beasts. The quality of the sculpture is of the highest order, and the figures show strong Hellenistic affinities. On the margins are inscribed, in runes, portions of the famous Old English poem, *The Dream of the Rood*, which has been ascribed to Caedmon.

Situation. At Ruthwell, 8½ miles east-south-east of Dumfries.

Admission. All times without charge.

DUNBARTONSHIRE

★*Dumbarton Castle*

Dumbarton Rock, a volcanic plug of basalt, has a longer recorded history as a stronghold than any other place in Britain. From at least the 5th century A.D. until 1018 it was the centre of the independent British kingdom of Strathclyde; in medieval Scotland it was an important royal castle; in more recent times Dumbarton's importance gradually declined, but it was garrisoned until the 20th century.

Dumbarton's Dark Age buildings and defences have been obliterated, and little survives from the Middle Ages. The most interesting structures are the fortifications of the 17th and 18th centuries, which illustrate a painful struggle by military engineers to adapt a problem site to contemporary defensive needs.

Situation. In Dumbarton.

Admission. Standard.

Admission Fee. 6*d.*

Official Guide Book. 1*s.*

Telephone No.: 473.

EAST LOTHIAN

★*Dirleton Castle*

One of the most beautiful ruins in Scotland, this ancient stronghold of the de Vaux stands amid a lovely flower-garden in the heart of the charming hamlet of Dirleton, the most English of Scottish villages. The castle had an eventful history from its first siege by Edward I in 1298 until its destruction by Lambert in 1650. The oldest work includes an imposing group of towers dating from the thirteenth century. These form, perhaps, the earliest known example of a clustered donjon. There is also much fine building of the fourteenth, fifteenth and sixteenth centuries. The castle crowns an igneous outcrop, and some of its lower chambers, including a "pit" or dungeon, are hewn out of the live rock. In the garden is a seventeenth century bowling green, surrounded by ancient yews.

Situation. In Dirleton.

Hours of Admission. Standard.

Admission Fee. 1*s.*

Official Guide Book. 1*s.*

Dunglass Collegiate Church

Founded in 1450 by Sir Alexander Hume for a provost, three chaplains, and four choir boys; consists of nave, choir, transepts, sacristy and a central tower. It is vaulted throughout, except in the tower, and the vaults, pointed in section, are covered with stone slabbed roofs. The interior embellishments are very rich. The church stands in the grounds of Dunglass House. It was held against the English in 1544, and in the eighteenth century was used as a stable.

Situation. Near Cockburnspath. 8 miles south-east of Dunbar.
Admission. All times without charge.

Haddington: St. Mary's Church

This fine cruciform church, formerly known as "the Lamp of Lothian," was the parish church of the ancient burgh of Haddington, and its nave is still so used, but the rest of the building is a ruin in the custody of the Ministry. The whole building dates from the fifteenth century and is one of the largest and moblest examples of Scottish ecclesiastical architecture of that period. The east walls of the transepts and the end walls of the choir aisles are windowless, a Scottish practice of the period. The flamboyant tracery of the large windows is exceptionally forceful and masculine, and the triple windows of the lofty tower form a landmark in the countryside. During the great siege of Haddington in 1548 the church suffered much, and narrowly escaped complete destruction. Its walls are still pitted with bullet marks.

Situation. In Haddington.
Admission. All times without charge.

Haddington: St. Martin's Church

The ruined nave of a Romanesque church, altered in the thirteenth century when the structure was vaulted and buttresses added. The chancel has disappeared.

Situation. In Haddington.
Admission. All times without charge.

★*Hailes Castle*

This beautiful ruin is of exceptional interest because its oldest portions date from before the War of Independence, and represent, not so much a castle as a fortified manor-house, closely resembling the well-known Aydon Castle in Northumberland. It then belonged to the Gourlays, but afterwards passed to the Hepburns, by whom a great square tower and high curtain walls were added. There is also a fine sixteenth century chapel. The castle was heavily involved in the War of the Rough Wooing, and was dismantled by Cromwell in 1650. It stands in a lovely situation on the bank of the Tyne.

Situation. Near East Linton.
Hours of Admission. Standard.
Admission Fee. *6d.*
Official Guide Pamphlet. *2d.*

Ormiston Market Cross, East Lothian

A fine free-standing fifteenth century cross, with a blank shield of arms, now erected on a modern base in the main street of the village.

Situation. About 3 miles south-south-east of Tranent.

Admission. All times without charge.

Preston Market Cross

One of the two surviving Scottish market crosses of its type, and the only one that still stands where and as it was built. It is a circular structure, with niches and a parapet, within which rises a tall shaft surmounted by a unicorn. Probably it was erected by the Hamiltons of Preston after they obtained the right to hold a fair in 1617.

Situation. About ½ mile inland from the coastal town of Prestonpans, near the main Edinburgh-North Berwick road.

Admission. All times without charge.

★Seton Collegiate Church

One of the most important ecclesiastical monuments in the near vicinity of Edinburgh. The church comprises a choir, north and south transepts and an unusual crossing tower of the type known as a broach tower. Foundations of the nave have recently been revealed during excavations. The nave was probably never erected, but the choir and transepts are complete. They are vaulted in stone and roofed with heavy stone slabs in a manner characteristic of this period. The church dates from the late fourteenth century. The collegiate foundation consisted of a provost, six prebendaries, one clerk and two singing boys.

Within are two first-class mural monuments in the Renaissance manner. At the east end is a fine arched mural tomb recess with two recumbent effigies of a Lord and his Lady, commemorating probably George, third Lord Seton, who was slain at Flodden in 1513, and his wife.

The monument is charmingly situated in well-wooded grounds. Nearby are the ruins of later domestic buildings.

Situation. 1 mile south-east of Cockenzie on the main Edinburgh-North Berwick road; near St. Germain's level crossing.

Hours of Admission. Standard.

Admission Fee. 1*s*.

★Tantallon Castle

This famous stronghold of the Douglases occupies a magnificent situation on the rocky coast of the Firth of Forth, opposite the Bass Rock. Although it has been the scene of stirring events, its historical renown is overmatched by the romantic glamour shed upon it through the part it plays in Scott's *Marmion*. The great frontal curtain wall, flanked by round towers and having an imposing central gatehouse, dates from the fourteenth century, and is one of the grandest things of its kind in Scotland. Outside the castle are extensive earthworks, some of which represent the defences thrown up against the cannon of James V, in 1526; while others, still further out, date from the Civil War. The impregnability of the castle in byegone times is suggested by an ancient rhyme:

"Ding down Tantallon—
Mak' a brig to the Bass!"

Situation. About 3 miles east of North Berwick.

Hours of Admission. Standard.

Admission Fee. 1*s.*

Official Guide. 1*s.* 6*d.*

FIFE

★*Aberdour Castle*

An extensive ruin overlooking Aberdour harbour. The oldest part is a rhomboidal tower of the fourteenth century, to which other buildings have been added *en échelon* by successive stages in the sixteenth and seventeenth centuries. Parts of the later buildings are still roofed. A terraced garden and bowling green may still be traced, and a fine circular dovecot remains in good preservation. Close by is the Norman parish church. King Robert Bruce granted the barony to his paladin, Randolph, Earl of Moray; later it belonged to the Douglases, Earls of Morton.

Situation. In Aberdour, on the Firth of Forth.

Hours of Admission. Standard.

Admission Fee. 1*s.*

Official Guide Book. 1*s.* 6*d.*

★*Culross Abbey*

This Cistercian monastery was founded by Malcolm, Earl of Fife, in 1217. There remains of it the choir, still used as the parish church, and parts, more or less, of the nave, the cellarium, the frater and the dorter. Only the south wall of the nave belongs to the early thirteenth century; the rest of the buildings date mostly from about 1300, and were again reconstructed in the reign of James IV. The rood screen and pulpitum are of particular interest. The fine central tower, still complete, bears the arms of Abbot Masoun (1498-1513). Culross was a daughter-house of Kinloss, in Moray. Latterly it fell into evil case, and at the Reformation there were no more than nine monks in residence.

Situation. In Culross, on the Firth of Forth.

Hours of Admission. Standard.

Admission Fee. 6*d.*

NOTE: Application to visit the church should be made at the Manse.

★*Culross, The Palace*

This charming mansion was built between 1597 and 1611 by George Bruce of Culross, a wealthy merchant who was knighted by James VI. Its crow-stepped gables, and pantiled roofs have long been a favourite subject with artists, while the painted ceilings are as fine as anything of their kind in Scotland. Adjoining the Palace is a terraced garden, gay with flowers.

Situation. At Culross, on the Firth of Forth.

Hours of Admission. Standard.

Admission Fee. 1*s.*

Dogton Stone

A much battered and weathered free-standing Celtic cross, with traces of animal and figure sculpture and interlaced and key-pattern ornament.

Situation. At Dogton farmhouse, 1½ miles east-north-east of Cardenden railway station.

Admission. All times without charge.

★*Dunfermline Abbey*

This great Benedictine house owes its foundation to the saintly Queen Margaret, and the foundations of her modest church remain beneath the present nave, which is a splendid piece of late Norman work, obviously by masons from Durham. The site of the choir is now occupied by a modern parish church, but at the east end of this the remains of St. Margaret's shrine, dating from the thirteenth century, are seen. King Robert Bruce is buried in the choir, his grave marked by a modern brass. Of the monastic buildings, the ruins of the frater, kitchen, pend and guest-house still remain, and are of much beauty and interest. The guest house was later reconstituted as a royal palace, and here Charles I was born.

Situation. In Dunfermline.

Hours of Admission. Standard, weekdays. Sundays, Summer only, 2.15-5.30. Without charge.

★*Inchcolm Abbey*

Sometimes described as "The Iona of the East," the remains of this monastery stand on a green island in the Firth of Forth. It was an Augustinian house, founded about 1123 by Alexander I. Caught in a gale, he was driven to Inchcolm, and took shelter in a hermit's chapel. This has been thought still to survive in a small and rude cell west of the abbey. The monastic buildings, which include a fine thirteenth century octagonal chapter house, are the best preserved in Scotland. The nave of the church is Norman, but it was gradually extended eastward, until a complete new cruciform church took the place of the early one, which was then converted into a dwelling house. In the original choir was discovered the finest example of thirteenth century wall-painting left in Scotland, showing a funeral procession of clerics. The abbey was much harried by English fleets, and the canons were frequently obliged to flee to the mainland. West of the abbey is a fine hog-backed stone.

Situation. In the Firth of Forth, opposite Aberdour.

Access. Motor boat transport from Aberdour should be arranged with local boat-hirer. Details of tides and availability of boat may be obtained from the Abbey custodian. (Aberdour 332).

Hours of Admission. Standard.

Admission Fee. 6d.

Official Guide Book. 1*s.*

Ravenscraig Castle

An imposing ruin on a rocky promontory between Dysart and Kirkcaldy. It was founded by James II in 1460, and the building accounts, extending to 1463, are in part preserved. Later the castle passed into the hands of the

Sinclair Earls of Orkney. It is remarkable both for the beauty of its ashlar masonry and also because it is perhaps the first British castle to be systematically designed for defence by fire-arms. The castle is the scene of Harold's piteous song about the fate of "Lovely Rosabelle" in his *Lay of the Last Minstrel.*

Situation. At the north end of the royal burgh of Kirkcaldy.

Admission. Work in progress: free admission during working hours.

Rosyth Castle and Dovecot

The castle consists of a square tower of sixteenth century date and buildings now ruinous, of a later age. The castle is in a good state of preservation and comprises three chambers, one upon another, served by a corner wheel stair rising from the ground floor. The additional buildings formed a courtyard round the original free-standing tower. The ground floor and the first floor of the tower are vaulted. The dovecot has a fine stone roof and gabled ends.

Situation. In Rosyth Dockyard.

Admission. On prior application to Ministry of Works, 122 George Street, Edinburgh, 2.

★*St. Andrews Castle*

This was the archiepiscopal castle of the primate of Scotland. Here Cardinal Beaton was murdered in 1546, and the first round of the Reformation struggle was fought out in the great siege that followed. The oldest parts of the extensive ruin date from the thirteenth century, but much of the work is later than the destruction of 1547. Notable features are the grim "Bottle-dungeon," and the mine and counter-mine tunnelled in the living rock during the siege. These works are unique in Britain. The castle stands on a promontory thrust out into the North Sea, and isolated by a deep and wide ditch.

Situation. In St. Andrews.

Hours of Admission. Standard.

Admission Fee. 1*s.* Including Bottle-dungeon and Subterranean Passage.

Official Guide Book. 1*s.*

★*St. Andrews Cathedral and Priory*

Of the metropolitan cathedral of Scotland, once the largest church in the country, with a length of 391 feet, little now remains save parts of the east and west gables, the south wall of the nave, and portions of the choir and south transept; but the foundations of the entire church have been recovered by excavation. The outline of the claustral buildings is also distinct, and considerable portions of the eastern and southern ranges still remain. Most of the surviving work belongs to the late twelfth and thirteenth centuries. The cathedral was also the church of a Priory of Augustinian Canons Regular. A large part of the precinct walls, including the Pends, or vaulted entrance passage, and a number of round towers, is still extant. This wall with its towers dates from the fourteenth century (see "Precincts and Pends"). In the cathedral museum is a magnificent collection of Celtic and medieval monuments, as well as pottery, glass work and other relics discovered on the site.

Situation. In St. Andrews.

Hours of Admission. Standard, without charge.

Official Guide Book. 1*s.* The Guide Book to Early Christian and Pictish Monuments of Scotland is also available. Price 5*s.*

St. Andrews: St. Rule's, or St. Regulus' Church

This was the first church of the Augustinian Canons, and was built by Bishop Robert (1126-59). It is by far the most interesting Romanesque church in Scotland. The remains consist of a choir and a western tower; the sanctuary and the later nave are gone. A feature of the building is its loftiness: the tower rises to a height of 108 feet. The masonry is megalithic; and in this and in the great height of the tower the church retains Celtic affinities, but the Romanesque detail has been shown to have been derived from the church of Wharran-le-Street, in Yorkshire.

Situation. In St. Andrews, within cathedral precincts.

Hours of Admission. Standard.

Admission Fee. 6*d.*, including museum.

Official Guide Book. Described in the Cathedral Guide.

St. Andrews: Precinct Wall and Pends

The precincts of the cathedral and priory of St. Andrews were some thirty acres in extent. They were enclosed by a high wall almost a mile in total length and fortified by projecting round towers disposed at intervals throughout. This precinct wall still stands about 25 feet high and is a prominent architectural feature at the east end of the town. The projecting towers are furnished with loops and carved heraldic panels, by which it has been attributed to Prior John Hepburn and his nephew and successor, Prior Patrick Hepburn, who held office in the cathedral in the sixteenth century. It is not unlikely, however, that there was a defensive wall encircling the precincts before this time and that the existing wall incorporates the ruins of its predecessor. The "Pends," is the stately ruin of a once-vaulted gatehouse to the cathedral precincts; fourteenth century; at the west end of the cathedral.

Situation. East end of St. Andrews surrounding the cathedral; fronting the Abbey Walk, the harbour, and the cliffs on the north side.

Admission. All times without charge.

Official Guide Book. Described in the Cathedral Guide.

St. Andrews: St. Mary's Church, Kirkheugh

The scanty foundations of a small cruciform church, on the edge of the cliff behind the cathedral. It is said to have been the church of the Culdee fraternity, and was pulled down by the Reformers in 1559.

Admission. All times without charge.

St. Andrews: Blackfriars Chapel

An apsidal, groin-vaulted aisle, built in 1525, is all that remains of this church.

Situation. South Street.

Admission. All times without charge.

St. Andrews: The West Port

This is one of the few surviving examples of a city gate in Scotland. Its building contract is dated 18th May, 1589, between Master David Russell, Dean of Guild, and Thomas Robertson, mason in Blebo. The Port was completely renovated in 1843 when some structural alterations were made. It now consists of a central archway protected from above by battling between two semi-octagonal turrets with gun-loops. On either side across the pavements is an arch of modern construction.

Situation. Across the west end of South Street.

Admission. All times without charge.

St. Bridget's Church, Dalgety

The old church forms the eastern part of the monument, which has to the west a later two-storey building comprising a burial vault on the ground floor with a "laird's loft" above, from which access was obtained to a western gallery within the church. The ancient church was dedicated to St. Bridget in 1244. The walls survive but are roofless. Later buildings have also been erected against the north wall, in the Renaissance style.

Situation. On the shores of the Forth, 2 miles south-west of Aberdour.

Admission. All times without charge.

Scotstarvit Tower

This fine tower is celebrated as the residence in the seventeenth century of Sir John Scot, author of *Scot of Scotstarvit's Staggering State of Scots Statesmen,* which Carlyle described as "a homily on life's nothingness enforced by examples." On its own merits, the tower is well worth a visit. Ashlar-faced, embattled and turreted, it rises to a height of five storeys and a garret, with roof and all complete. The two main apartments are vaulted. An armorial panel is dated 1627, but the tower is known to have been in existence in 1579. It stands on high ground, and is a notable landmark.

Situation. 3 miles south of Cupar, on the Cupar-Kennoway road.

Admission. All reasonable times without charge on application to custodian.

HEBRIDES: for monuments in the Hebrides see under Inverness-shire, and Ross and Cromarty.

INVERNESS-SHIRE

★Beauly Priory

One of the three monastic houses of the Valliscaulian Order founded in Scotland—all in the same year, 1230. The other two were Pluscarden in Moray and Ardchattan in Argyll (see *supra*, p. 75). Nothing but the church remains above ground. It is a long narrow building, comprising an aisleless nave, transepts, and chancel. The plan is extremely interesting, as it represents the earliest form of Cistercian church in Britain. Much of the building was reconstructed in the fourteenth-sixteenth centuries, and a north chapel was added to the nave. The architecture of all periods is very beautiful. The north transept now forms the burial place of the Mackenzies of Kintail, and contains the fine monument of Sir Kenneth Mackenzie (*d.* 1541).

Situation. In Beauly.

Hours of Admission. Standard, without charge.

Official Guide Pamphlet. 3*d.*

Clava Cairns

A group of burial cairns in which three concentric rings of great stones are now the principal features exposed; of late Neolithic or Early Bronze Age date.

Situation. 6 miles east of Inverness, on the right bank of the River Nairn. Opposite Culloden battlefield.

Admission. All times without charge.

Corriemony Chambered Cairn

Megalithic chambered cairn, probably Neolithic, surrounded by a peristalith of stone slabs, outside which is a circle of 11 standing stones. Access was by a low passage to the central circular chamber which contained a single crouched burial.

Situation. Glen Urquhart, 8½ miles west of Drumnadrochit.

Admission. All times without charge.

Glenelg Brochs: Dun Telve and Dun Troddan

Two Iron Age broch towers, ruinous but with wall portions still standing over 30 feet in height. Entrances, galleries, courts and other structural features well preserved.

Situation. On the west coast of Inverness-shire about 10 miles south of Kyle of Lochalsh, on the roadside.

Admission. All times without charge.

Inverlochy Castle

A fine and well-preserved example of a thirteenth century castle of the Comyns, with a quadrangular wall and round angle towers displaying the characteristic long bow-slits of the period. One of the towers, larger than the rest, forms the donjon. The castle has an eventful history dating from the War of Independence, and was the scene of Nontrose's great victory over the Campbells on 2nd February, 1645.

Situation. 2 miles north-east of Fort William.

Admission. Not yet open to the public. May be viewed from outside.

Knocknagael Boar Stone

A roughly shaped slab. At the top is incised the mirror-case symbol and below the figure of a wild boar. The round part of the mirror case is ornamented with a circle and a central dot and the boar has spiral curves on the body.

Situation. Almost opposite Burnside House in a field on Knocknagel Farm: close to the road, 3 miles south of Inverness railway station.

Admission. All times without charge.

Rodel: St. Clement's Church

The only cruciform medieval church in the Outer Isles. It was built by Alasdair Crottach MacLeod, eighth chief of Dunvegan Castle, in Skye, and contains his stately tomb, in which he was buried in 1547. The rich decoration of the church has obviously been derived from the work at Iona, and like the latter, betrays strong Irish influence. Some fine grave slabs of the late West Highland pattern may be seen in the churchyard.

Situation. At Rodel, in the Isle of Harris.

Admission. All reasonable times without charge on application to custodian.

★*Urquhart Castle*

One of the largest castles in Scotland, this extensive ruin occupies a commanding situation on a promontory jutting forth into Loch Ness, and must have been even more imposing before the level of the water was raised. Occupying the site of a vitrified fort, the castle began as a *motte* with a double bailey, the defences of which were rehabilitated in stone during the fourteenth century. Most of the existing buildings, however, including the gate-house and the upper part of the great square tower, date from after the Chiefs of Grant got possession of the castle in 1509. It has played a great part in Scottish history from the invasion of Edward I until the Jacobite rising of 1689, after which it was blown up.

Situation. On Loch Ness, near Drumnadrochit.

Hours of Admission. Standard.

Admission Fee. *6d.*

Official Guide Pamphlet. *3d.*

KINROSS-SHIRE

Burleigh Castle

A fine tower-house dating from about 1500, roofless but otherwise almost intact, to which there is still attached the fore-curtain of the barmkin or courtyard enclosure with an entrance flanked by gun-loops, and a picturesque angle tower, corbelled out above with a square cap-house, still roofed. The cap-house is dated 1582. This was the seat of the ancient family of Balfour of Burleigh. Lying on the main road through Fife and Kinross, the castle was several times visited by James VI on his northern progresses.

Situation. 1 mile east of Milnathort on the Leslie road.

Admission. All reasonable times without charge on application to key-keeper at farm opposite.

Loch Leven Castle

Consists of a tower of late fourteenth or early fifteenth century date standing on one side of an irregular courtyard enclosed by a curtain wall of later date, probably sixteenth century. This curtain, however, embodies some older masonry, probably of the castle besieged by the English in 1325. At one angle of the curtain is a projecting circular four-storeyed tower with gun-loops. The tower is oblong on plan and contains five storeys.

Mary Queen of Scots was imprisoned in the castle in 1567 and from it escaped a year later.

The castle can be seen across the waters of the loch from the main Edinburgh-Perth road, before entering Kinross.

Situation. On an island in Loch Leven.

Admission. No official facilities for transport to the island; visitors are advised to consult the local boatman. Admission at all reasonable times without charge.

KIRKCUDBRIGHTSHIRE

★*Cardoness Castle*

This ancient home of the McCullochs stands on a rocky platform above the Water of Fleet. It is a fine and well-preserved fifteenth century tower-house, four storeys in height, with a vaulted basement. The fireplaces in the great hall and the upper hall or solar are particularly good. Remains of outer defences still exist.

Situation. One mile south-west of Gatehouse of Fleet; on the main Gatehouse-Newton-Stewart road.

Hours of Admission. Standard.

Admission Fee. 6d.

Cairn Holy

Two cairns which belong to the Galloway group of Clyde-Carlingford chambared tombs. The entrances had been blocked by large stones which subsequently fell or were pulled forward. Excavations showed that the earlier usage was associated with Neolithic pottery and that there was a second phase represented by the presence of Beaker fragments (ca. 1800 B.C.).

Situation. 6½ miles S.E. of Creetown.

Admission. All times without charge.

Carsluith Castle

A roofless sixteenth century tower-house on the L-plan, which differs from most buildings of this class in that the staircase wing or "jamb" is an addition, dated 1568. The original square tower had an open parapet with angle turrets. This castle belonged to the Browns of Carsluith, and one of its owners was the last abbot of Sweetheart Abbey.

Situation. 3½ miles south-south-east of Creetown, overlooking Wigtown Bay, on the main Gatehouse-Newton Stewart road.

Admission. All reasonable times without charge, on application to custodian.

Drumcoltran Tower

The building is oblong on plan, three storeys high with a garret storey in the roof, all served by a wheel or spiral stair in a projecting square stair tower or wing: a good example of a Scottish tower house of about the middle of the sixteenth century. It is simple and severe; has a slightly overhanging parapet wall supported on projecting corbels. The gables of the typical saddle-backed roof are set back from the parapet wall.

Situation. Among farm buildings, 7 miles north-east of Dalbeattie.

Admission. All times without charge.

★*Dundrennan Abbey*

This Cistercian house was founded by David I and Fergus, Lord of Galloway, in 1142, and was colonized from Rievaulx. Here Mary Queen of Scots spent her last night on her native soil, before seeking shelter in England. The ruins, which are considerable and of great beauty, include much late Norman and Transitional work, and a rich chapter-house dating from the end of the thirteenth century. Of the church, little but the west end and the transepts now remains. The western claustral range is fairly well preserved, but of the southern little remains. Among the ruins are preserved many fine monuments, including a rather gruesome one of an abbot who had been murdered, possibly by a native Gallovidian who disliked the incoming Latin monks.

Situation. 6½ miles south-east of Kirkcudbright.

Hours of Admission. Standard.

Admission Free. *6d.*

Official Guide Pamphlet. *2d.*

★*Maclellan's Castle, Kircudbright*

This handsome castellated mansion was built after 1577 by Sir Thomas Maclellan of Bombie, it is said out of the stones of the Greyfriars convent in Kirkcudbright. A heraldic group over the door bears the date 1582. The house is elaborately planned, and its architectural details are particularly fine. It has been a ruin since 1752. Its builder was Provost of Kirkcudbright, and his fine late Gothic or early Renaissance altar tomb remains in the Old Greyfriars Kirk.

Situation. In the centre of the town.

Hours of Admission. Standard.

Admission Fee. *6d.*

★*Orchardton Tower*

An example, unique in Scotland, of a tower house on the cylindrical plan. It was built by John Cairns about the middle of the fifteenth century, and in other respects its arrangements do not differ from those of the normal rectangular tower-houses of that time. The first floor room served both as hall and chapel. There are some remnants of outbuildings.

Situation. 6 miles south-east of Castle Douglas.

Admission. All reasonable times without charge on application to custodian.

★*Sweetheart Abbey*

One of the most beautiful monastic ruins in Scotland, and famous because of the touching circumstances of its foundation, by Dervorgilla, Lady of Galloway, in memory of her husband, John Balliol, the founder of Balliol College, Oxford. The foundation dates from 1273, and in 1289 the foundress was buried in front of the high altar, with the "sweet heart" of her lord resting on her bosom. The monks were Cistercians, brought from Dundrennan. A remarkable feature of the ruins is the well-preserved precinct wall, enclosing 30 acres, and built of enormous boulders—no doubt cleared off the ground by the monks when they prepared the site for their convent. Little remains but the church, whose central tower is a conspicuous landmark. Much of the work dates from the early fourteenth century, a troublous period that saw little building in Scotland, so that the Sweetheart ruins are of special interest to the ecclesiologist.

Situation. At New Abbey, 7 miles south of Dumfries.

Hours of Admission. Standard.

Admission Fee. 1*s.*

Official Guide Book. 1*s.*

**Threave Castle*

This mighty tower of the "Black Douglases" stands on a lonely islet in the River Dee. It was built towards the end of the fourteenth century by Archibald the Grim, third Earl of Douglas and Lord of Galloway. The tower, which is four storeys high, is enclosed by an outer wall, with round towers loop-holed for firearms. This dates from 1513, in the crisis that followed Flodden. The castle was dismantled after its capture by the Covenanters in 1640.

Situation. 3 miles west of Castle Douglas.

Hours of Admission. Open April to September. Standard, but closed on Thursdays.

Admission Fee. 6*d.*

Official Guide Pamphlet. 2*d.*

LANARKSHIRE

**Bothwell Castle* (Plates 14 & 15.)

This was the largest and finest stone castle in Scotland dating from before the War of Independence, though the full design seems never to have been completed. It was the principal English base in western Scotland during the Plantagenet occupation, and was repeatedly taken and retaken. The chief remnant of the original structure is the superb cylindrical donjon, one half of which was cast down by the Scots when they finally retook the castle in 1336. Later it belonged to the Douglases, to whom its reconstruction is due. The Douglas buildings include a hall and a chapel, both in very rich architecture. The castle is grandly situated on a steep bank overlooking a bend of the River Clyde, and stands in a spacious and well-timbered park. Near it are the fifteenth century Bothwell Church and Bothwell Bridge, where the Covenanters were defeated by Monmouth in 1679.

Situation. Nr. Uddingston, in the southern outskirts of Glasgow.

Hours of Admission. Standard.

Admission Fee. 6*d.*

Official Guide Pamphlet. 2*d.*

Official Guide Book. 1*s.* 6*d.*

Coulter Motte Hill

A good example of the Norman castle mound, originally moated and surmounted by a palisade enclosing a timber tower (see page 59).

Situation. At Coulter Railway Station.

Admission. All times without charge.

Craignethan Castle

This extensive and well-preserved ruin, famous as the "Tillietudlem" of Scott's *Old Mortality*, has a genuine history of much importance in the religious wars of the sixteenth century, when, as chief stronghold of the Hamiltons, supporters of Queen Mary, it was repeatedly assailed by the Protestant party, and partly dismantled by them in 1579. The oldest and central portion is a large tower house of an unusual design, and very ornate in its details. This was built by Sir James Hamilton of Finnart, the favourite of James V. The outer walls and towers are exceptionally well preserved. The castle occupies a highly romantic situation, almost hidden away in an umbrageous dell ovelooking the Nethan.

Situation. 5½ miles west-north-west of Lanark.

Admission. Work in progress; free admittance during working hours.

**Glasgow Cathedral*

The only complete medieval cathedral surviving on the Scottish mainland. It is remarkable for the ambulatory that runs all round the building, thus providing for the traffic of pilgrims to the shrine of St. Mungo (Kentigern), placed in a crypt or lower church under the eastern limb, where the ground falls. The cathedral comprises an aisled nave, aisled choir and presbytery, dwarf transepts and a central tower crowned with a lofty stone spire. The two western towers have unhappily been removed. Externally the great church seems somewhat austere, but this is amply compensated by the glories of the interior. The presbytery dates from the thirteenth century, the nave was built about 1300, and the tower a century later. In 1484 the Blacader aisle was attached to the south transept. Notable features in this splendid building are the elaborate vaulting in the crypt, the fourteenth century timber roof, and the stone screen or pulpitum of the fifteenth century. At the north east corner is the sacristy, completed in the fifteenth century in the manner of a castle.

Situation. In Cathedral Square off Castle Street.

Admission. Weekdays April-May 10 a.m. — 3.30 p.m.
June-Sept. 10 a.m. — 6 p.m.
Oct.-March 10 a.m. — 4.30 p.m.

Sundays April-Sept. 2.30-5 p.m. only. Without charge.

St. Bride's Church, Douglas

All that remains of this church is the unaisled choir and the south side of the nave. The choir contains three fine altar-tombs of the great Douglas family, whose principal shrine this was. These monuments, which, with the choir itself, have been restored, commemorate the "Good Sir James," Bruce's paladin; Archibald, fifth Earl of Douglas and Duke of Touraine; and "James the Gross," seventh Earl, with his lady. Some loose fragments of the pre-existing Norman church are extant.

Situation. In Douglas.

Admission. All reasonable times without charge, on application to custodian.

MIDLOTHIAN

Castle Law Fort, Glencorse

A small Iron Age hill fort consisting of two concentric banks and ditches. In the older rock-cut ditch a souterrain or earth-house is preserved. The site was occupied into Roman times (second century A.D.).

Situation. On the summit of Castle-Knowe, a small hill on the south-eastern slope of the Pentland Hills, about 1 mile from Glencorse village.

Admission. All reasonable times without charge on application to key-keeper in nearby cottage.

**Crichton Castle*

One of the largest and finest of Scottish castles, standing on a bare and lofty site overlooking the River Tyne. The nucleus is a plain fourteenth century tower-house, to which a group of buildings, dating variously from the fifteenth-seventeenth centuries, has been added, so as to form a quadrangular mansion, enclosing a narrow courtyard. The most spectacular feature of these additions is an arcaded range, the upper frontage of which is wrought with faceted stone-work, well described in Scott's *Marmion:*

> *"Still rises unimpaired below*
> *The courtyard's graceful portico*
> *Above its cornice, row and row*
> *Of fair hewn facets richly show*
> *Their pointed diamond form."*

This work, in the Italianate manner, was erected by the Earl of Bothwell between 1581 and 1591. He had been in Italy, and probably had seen the Palazzo dei Diamanti at Ferrara. Near the castle is the fine fifteenth century parish church.

Situation. 3 miles east of Gorebridge.

Hours of Admission. Standard; but closed on Fridays, October to May.

Admission Fee. 6d.

Official Guide Book. 1*s.*

**Edinburgh Castle*

The most famous of Scottish castles, and now additionally celebrated because it contains the Scottish National Memorial of the First World War. The walls which enclose the summit of the mighty basalt rock retain some medieval work, but mostly belong to the seventeenth and eighteenth centuries: the Half Moon Battery was built by the Regent Morton, and encloses the remains of the great tower built by David II and destroyed by English guns in the siege of 1573. The oldest building on the rock is St. Margaret's Chapel, a small example of Norman work. The Great Hall, built by James IV, retains its fine open timber roof. The royal apartments still show much of their painted decoration. Here are preserved the Regalia or crown jewels of Scotland. In front of St. Margaret's Chapel stands the famous fifteenth century bombard, Mons Meg.

Hours of Admission

Summer Hours (June-September inclusive):

Week-days	9.30 a.m. — 6 p.m.	(All apartments).
	6.00 p.m. — 9 p.m.	(Precincts only).
Sundays	11.00 a.m. — 6 p.m.	(All apartments).
	6.00 p.m. — 9 p.m.	(Precincts only).

Hours are slightly shorter at other times of the year and details may be obtained by telephoning the number below.

Admission Fee. 1*s*. (War Memorial and Precincts Free).

Official Guide Book. 1*s*. 6*d*.

Popular Guide Book. 1*s*. 6*d*. *Folder Guide* (English and French). 4*d*.

Souvenir Guide Book to Scottish United Services Museum. 9*d*.

Telephone No.: Edinburgh, Caledonian 6784.

Edinburgh: Corstorphine Dovecot

A fine dovecot in a good state of preservation, with nesting boxes within; circular on plan; dates from the seventeenth century.

Situation. In the suburb of Corstorphine (Dovecot Road).

Admission. All times without charge.

★*Edinburgh: Craigmillar Castle*

This renowned castle, whose fame and form are familiar to Scotsmen all the world over, is forever associated with some of the darkest and most tragic episodes in the career of Queen Mary. Its great central fourteenth century tower, built by the Prestons, was enclosed in the early part of the next century by an embattled curtain wall, and within this are stately ranges of apartments dating from the sixteenth and seventeenth centuries. The castle was burned by Hereford in 1544. Within its walls, in 1567, and while the Queen herself was in residence, the "Craigmillar band," as the plot to murder Darnley was called, was signed by some of her nobles. The outbuildings of the castle include an interesting chapel.

Situation. In Edinburgh; southern suburbs.

Hours of Admission. Standard.

Admission Fee. 6*d*.

Official Guide Book. 1*s*.

★*Edinburgh: Holyrood Abbey and Palace of Holyroodhouse*

The Abbey of Holyrood was founded by David I for Augustinian Canons regular. All that remains of the monastic buildings is the ruined nave of the Abbey church. This has been probably the finest piece of sheer design in the thirteenth century ecclesiastical architecture of Scotland. Foundations of King David's church exist on the site of the later chancel. The oldest part of the Palace, which is built against the monastic nave, is the north-west tower, erected by James IV. The rest of the quadrangular building was reconstructed, in the neo-classical style, by the famous architect, Sir William

Bruce, to the order of Charles II. James IV's Tower still retains the rooms for ever associated with the tragic happenings of which the Palace of Holyroodhouse became the scene in Queen Mary's reign.

Situation. At the foot of the Canongate.

Hours of Admission

Summer Hours (June-September inclusive):
  Weekdays 9.30 a.m. — 6 p.m.
  Sundays 11.00 a.m. — 6 p.m.

Hours are slightly shorter at other times of the year and details may be obtained by telephoning the number below.

Admission Fee. Historical and State Apartments. 1*s.*

Official Guide Book. 1*s.*

Popular Guide Book. 1*s.* 6*d.* *Folder Guide* (English and French). 4*d.*

Telephone No.: Edinburgh Waverley 1847.

Edinburgh: St. Triduana's Chapel, Restalrig Collegiate Church

According to legend, St. Triduana in the eighth century plucked out her eyes to confound King Nechtan of the Picts who had professed an importunate love; she thereafter retired to Restalrig, where she was buried. Her shrine became a place of pilgrimage for those who were afflicted with diseases of the eye. From the late fifteenth century the shrine was situated in the lower chamber of the king's chapel built by James III adjacent to Restalrig church. The design, a two-storeyed vaulted hexagon, is unique. The lower chapel of St. Triduana survives intact; it was restored in 1907-8 after use a as burial-vault. The upper chamber, a chapel of unknown dedication, was demolished in 1560.

Situation. Restalrig district, east side of Edinburgh.

Admission. Not yet open to the public. May be closely viewed from the churchyard.

MORAY

Burghead Well

This remarkable rock-cut structure, within the *murus Gallicus* of an Iron Age fort, is probably an early Christian baptistery, associated with the local *cultus* of St. Ethan. The locality is famous for the number of stones with figures of bulls, incised in the style of the oldest Pictish symbols, that it has yielded.

Situation. At Burghead.

Admission. All times without charge.

Duffus Castle

The original seat of the de Moravia or Murray family, now represented by the ducal houses of Atholl and Sutherland. This is the finest example of a mount and bailey castle in the north of Scotland, and is unique by reason of the wide outer precinct ditch, enclosing eight acres, which surrounds the castle. About 1300 the bailey was walled in, and a great stone tower, of very fine workmanship, was erected on the mount, which has slipped under its weight, splitting the tower in two. Within the curtain are remains of a hall, reconstructed in the fifteenth century.

Situation. 5 miles north-west of Elgin.

Admission. All reasonable times without charge on application to key-keeper, Mr. A. A. Gill, Old Duffus, Duffus, Elgin.

Official Guide Pamphlet. 2*d.* (Available at Elgin Cathedral).

Duffus: St. Peter's Church and Parish Cross

Duffus Church retains the base of a fourteenth century western tower, a fine vaulted porch of the sixteenth century, and some interesting tomb-stones.
The Parish Cross, a tall and elegant cross shaft apparently of fourteenth century date, about 14 feet high, stands upon its original stepped base. An enriched band girdles the shaft near the top: the cross head is much weathered.

Situation. Duffus churchyard.

Admission. All times without charge.

**Elgin Cathedral* (Plates 16 & 17.)

When entire, this was perhaps the most beautiful of our Scottish cathedrals. The remains consist of a nave with double aisles and north and south porches; twin western towers having a superb portal and window between; transepts, above which rose a great central tower, now gone; choir with aisles and presbytery; and a detached octagonal chapter-house. The cathedral was founded in 1224, and much of the remaining work is in the high and rich style of that century: but in 1390 the church was burned by the "Wolf of Badenoch," and the ruins thus show traces of extensive reconstruction subsequent to this catastrophe. The early work betrays strong French influence. The chapter-house, reconstructed in the fifteenth century, is the finest thing of its kind in Scotland. In the surviving ruins, and in the detached fragments assembled on the site, there is a wealth of moulded work, heraldic decoration, and figure sculpture, forming a notable conspectus of the medieval mason-craftsman's art. Preserved in the nave is a fine Celtic cross-slab, with Pictish symbols.

Situation. In Elgin.

Hours of Admission. Standard.

Admission Fee. 1*s.*

Official Guide Book. 1*s.* 6*d.*

Elgin: Bishop's House

A small remnant of the town house of the Bishops of Moray immediately opposite Elgin Cathedral. It now forms a picturesque ruin, and possesses some pleasing architectural features, notably a fine oriel window. The crow steps of the gables are themselves gabled. Coats of arms on the building include those of Bishop Patrick Hepburn (1535-73) and Robert Reid, Abbot of Kinloss and Bishop of Orkney (1541-58). The oldest stone is dated 1557.

Admission. Not yet open to the public.

Sueno's Stone (Plate 12.)

One of the most remarkable early sculptured monuments in Scotland; 20 feet high. On one side a tall cross accompanied by once elaborate figure sculpture at the base; on the other sculptured groups of figures of warriors, etc., disposed as though depicting hunting and warlike scenes.

Situation. In Forres, east end of town.

Admission. All times without charge.

NAIRNSHIRE

Ardclach Bell Tower

The tower is but 14 feet square and contains two storeys. A straight stone stair leads from the vaulted ground floor to the upper floor. This has a fireplace, on either side of which is a square gun-loop with well-splayed openings towards the interior, and a square aperture to the exterior. The side gable is also equipped with a small gun-loop. The apex of this gable is surmounted by a small belfry wherein was housed the bell which summoned the worshippers to the Parish Church of Ardclach nearby, and doubtless, also, as may be inferred from the prominent position of this little structure, gave warning to the neighbourhood in cases of alarm. The tower stands on the summit of a lofty promontory above the River Findhorn and it is thought to have been erected in the middle of the seventeenth century. There are a few detached belfries in Scotland but none quite like this, with its two little cjambers and gun-loops and small windows for the use of watchmen.

Situation. 8½ miles south-east of Nairn.

Admission. All reasonable times, on application to custodian.

THE ORKNEY ISLANDS

NOTE:

Monuments on the mainland are easily accessible. St. Peter's Church, Birsay, is on a tidal island. Crossing is impossible during the period approximately 3 hours before High Water to 3 hours after. High Water is 1 hour before High Water Kirkwall, which is intimated at the Harbourmaster's office there. There are no crossings by boat. The intending visitor to monuments on the islands of Egilsay, Etnhallow, Rousay and Wyre is advised to arrange beforehand, for motor-boat transport, with Mr. Magnus Flaws, Telephone Wyre 203. The key-keeper and official guide to the Rousay monuments is Mr. Hourie, Telephone Wasbister 2, whom it is advisable to warn of a proposed visit.

Visitors to Sanday, Westray, Papa Westray and the Holm of Papa Westray should consult the steamer time-table. Steamers leave from Kirkwall.

The key-keeper of the Holm of Papa Westray is Mr. John Rendall, Cuppins, Papa Westray.

The attention of visitors is drawn to the comprehensive Official Guide Book to Orkney monuments; obtainable from the Stationery Office and at the principal monuments on the Orkney Mainland, etc. Price 2*s.* 6*d.*

MAINLAND

Click Mill, Dounby

The only working example of the old Orcadian horizontal water-mills.

Situation. At Dounby.

Admission. All times without charge.

Official Guide Pamphlet 2*d.* (Available at Earl's Palace, Kirkwall).

Cuween Hill Chambered Cairn

A low mound covering a megalithic passage tomb. The main chamber contains four mural cells. Contained the bones of men, dogs and oxen when discovered. Of Neolithic date (*c.* 2000 B.C.).

Situation. About ½ mile south of Finstown.

Finstown is approximately 7 miles west-north-west of Kirkwall.

Admission. All reasonable times without charge, on application to key-keeper at nearby farmhouse.

Earth-house Grain

A well-built Iron Age souterrain or earth-house comprising entrance stair, passage and underground chamber; the roof is supported by stone pillars.

Situation. About 1 mile north-west of the town of Kirkwall: within the boundaries of Hatston airfield.

Admission. All reasonable times without charge, on application to key-keeper at 38 Hatston Houses, Kirkwall.

★*Gurness—The Broch of* (Plate 9.)

An Iron Age broch tower still standing over 10 feet high surrounded by a complex of secondary huts and other buildings, the whole encircled by a deep rock-cut ditch. The site was later inhabited in Dark Age and Viking times.

Situation. At Aikerness, near Evie, about 14 miles north west of Kirkwall

Bus tours arranged periodically in season.

Hours of Admission. Standard.

Admission Fee. 6*d.*

Official Guide Pamphlet. 3*d.*

★*Kirkwall: The Bishop's Palace*

An extensive ruin closely adjoining the Cathedral. The main portion consists of a hall-house dating originally from the twelfth century, but much altered subsequently, in particular by Bishop Reid (1541-8) who added a powerful round tower, embattled and pierced for guns. A still later addition was made by Patrick Stewart, Earl of Orkney, about 1600.

Admission. See under Earl's Palace.

★*Kirkwall: Earl Patrick's Palace*

This magnificent building, which stands, roofless but otherwise almost complete, immediately opposite the Bishop's Palace, has been well described as "the most mature and accomplished piece of Renaissance architecture left in Scotland." It forms three sides of a square, and is distinguished by the ability of its planning and the masterly refinement of its architectural details. Notable features are the great oriel windows, in the French manner. The palace was built by Earl Patrick Stewart between 1600 and 1607, but the full design was never completed.

Admission Fee. 6*d.* (Including Bishop's Palace).

	Weekdays	*Sundays*
April—September	10 a.m.—7 p.m.	2 p.m.—7 p.m.
October—March	10 a.m.—Dusk.	2 p.m.—Dusk.

Official Guide Pamphlet. 3*d.*

★*Maes Howe Chambered Cairn* (Plates 5 & 6.)

The finest megalithic tomb in the British Isles, the masonry being unsurpassed in Western Europe. A large mound covers a stone-built passage and large corbelled burial chamber with mural cells; of Neolithic date (*c.* 2000 B.C.): plundered in Viking times. Norse runes are inscribed on several stones.

Situation. About 9 miles west of Kirkwall on the main Kirkwall to Stromness road. Bus service.

Admission:	*Weekdays*	*Sundays*
April—September	All reasonable	2 p.m.—7 p.m.
October—March	times	2 p.m.—4 p.m.

Apply to key-keeper in nearby farmhouse.

Admission Fee. 6*d.*

Official Guide Pamphlet. 3*d.*

★*Onston, or Unstan, Chambered Cairn*

An almost circular mound bounded by three concentric walls and covering a megalithic burial chamber divided by upright slabs into five compartments; of Neolithic or Stone Age date (*c.* 2000 B.C.). Fragments of over 22 pottery bowls of a type now known as the Unstan class of Neolithic pottery were found in the chamber.

Situation. About 3½ miles north-north-east of Stromness on the Stromness-Kirkwall road.

Admission. All reasonable times without charge, on application to key-keeper.

Orphir: St. Nicholas' Church

Only the chancel and a small part of the nave remain of this, the single example of a round church known to have been built in the Middle Ages in Scotland. The structure dates from the twelfth century, and appears to have been modelled on Scandinavian prototypes, derived ultimately from the Church of the Holy Sepulchre at Jerusalem.

Situation. 8 miles west-south-west of Kirkwall on the north shore of Scapa Flow.

Admission. All times without charge.

Orphir: The Earl's Bu

The partly excavated foundations of ancient buildings which may be an Earl's palace of Viking times mentioned in the *Orkneyinga Saga.*

Situation. Adjacent to St. Nicholas' church.

Admission. All times without charge.

Rennibister Earth-house

An excellent example of the Orkney type of Iron Age souterrain or earth-house consisting of a passage and underground chamber with supporting roof-pillars.

Situation. About 4½ miles west-north-west of Kirkwall. On the Kirkwall to Finstown road.

Admission. All reasonable times without charge, on application to key-keeper in farmhouse.

Ring of Brogar Stone Circle (Plate 4.)

A magnificent circle of upright stones with enclosing ditch spanned by causeways; of Bronze Age date.

Situation. On the north-east shore of Loch of Stenness about 5 miles north-east of Stromness.

Admission. All times without charge.

Ring of Stenness Stone Circle

The remains of a stone circle standing on a mound or platform encircled by a ditch and bank. Of Bronze Age date.

Situation. Situated on the southern shore of the Loch of Harray about 5 miles north-east of Stromness.

Admission. All times without charge.

★*Skara Brae: Prehistoric Village* (Plates 1, 2 & 3.)

An impressive cluster of Stone Age dwellings preserved in drift sand. The dwellings—rectangular rooms with rounded corners—and passages are amazingly conserved with their stone furniture, hearths and drains.

Situation. On the west coast: Bay of Skaill.

From Kirkwall, 19 miles north-west, and from Stromness 7 miles to the north.

Hours of Admission. Standard.

Admission Fee. 1*s.*

Official Guide Book. Price 1*s.*

★*St. Peter's Church, Birsay*

On this tidal island stands a ruined Romanesque church, consisting of nave chancel and semicircular apse, with claustral buildings appended on the north side. No record of the monastery has survived. A magnificent sculptured stone, with Pictish symbols and three warriors in procession, was discovered in the ruins and is now in the National Museum. Close beside the church, remains of Viking dwellings have been unearthed and are now conserved.

Situation. At Birsay, north end of Mainland, 20 miles north-west of Kirkwall.

Admission. All times without charge. Crossings by foot except at high water. No crossings by boat.

Official Guide Book. The Early Christian and Norse Settlements, Birsay. Price 1*s.* (Available at major monuments in Orkney).

Wideford Hill Chambered Cairn

A conspicuous megalithic chambered cairn with three concentric walls. The burial chamber with three large cells leading off it is entered by a passage; of Neolithic date (*c.* 2000 B.C.).

Situation. About 2 miles west of Kirkwall.

Admission. All reasonable times without charge, on application to the key-keeper.

ISLAND OF EGILSAY

St. Magnus Church

This remarkable structure, roofless but otherwise almost entire, consists of a nave, a square-ended and vaulted chancel, and a western tower, the latter being tall and cylindrical, somewhat after the manner of the Celtic round towers such as those at Brechin and Abernethy. Above the chancel vault there was a room. A church existed here in 1116, when St. Magnus was martyred either in the building or just outside it. It seems probable, however, that the existing structure dates from nearer the end of that century.

Admission. All reasonable times without charge, key from nearby farmhouse.

ISLAND OF EYNHALLOW

Eynhallow Church

A twelfth century church, consisting of nave, chancel and west porch, all greatly altered and now much ruined. Close by is a group of domestic buildings, likewise much ruined. A monastery is known to have existed on the island, but it is doubtful whether any of its remains can be recognized in the surviving ruins.

Admission. All times without charge.

ISLAND OF HOY

Dwarfie Stane

A huge block of sandstone in which a Neolithic burial chamber has been quarried resembling the rock-cut chambered tombs common in the Mediterranean, Portugal, and other parts of the Atlantic megalithic province. No other tomb of this type is known in the British Isles. Of Neolithic date (*c.* 2000 B.C.).

Situation. On the island of Hoy: centre; north end.

Admission. All times without charge. Access by boat from Stromness.

ISLAND OF ROUSAY

Blackhammer Chambered Cairn

A long cairn bounded by a well-preserved retaining wall and containing a megalithic burial chamber divided into seven compartments or stalls; of Neolithic date (*c.* 2000 B.C.).

Situation. On the west coast.

Admission. All reasonable times without charge.

Knowe of Yarso Chambered Cairn

An oval cairn with concentric casing walls enclosing a megalithic chambered tomb divided by paired upright slabs into three compartments or stalls; of Neolithic date (*c.* 2000 B.C.).

Situation. On the west coast.

Admission. All reasonable times without charge.

Mid Howe Broch

An Iron Age broch tower and walled enclosure situated on a promontory cut off by a deep rock-cut ditch. The court-like enclosure contains secondary buildings.

Situation. On the west coast.

Admission. All reasonable times without charge.

Mid Howe Chambered Cairn (Plate 7.)

An impressive megalithic chambered tomb contained in an oval barrow with three concentric casing walls. The chamber is divided into 12 compartments containing stone slab benches; of Neolithic date (*c.* 2000 B.C.).

Situation. Near Mid Howe Broch.

Admission. All reasonable times without charge.

Taversöe Tuick Chambered Cairn

A megalithic chambered burial mound containing two burial chambers divided into stalls; of Neolithic date (*c.* 200 B.C.).

Situation. On the west coast.

Admission. All reasonable times without charge.

ISLAND OF SANDAY

Quoyness Chambered Cairn

A megalithic chambered cairn with triple retaining walls containing a passage and main chamber with six beehive cells; of Neolithic date (*c.* 2000 B.C.).

Situation. At Quoy Ness.

Admission. All reasonable times without charge, on application to key-keeper at Elsness Farm. Islands steamer service from Kirkwall.

ISLAND OF WESTRAY

★Noltland Castle

A fine ruin on the Z-plan, with square towers at each of two diagonally opposite corners. This castle is remarkable for its tiers of yawning gun-loops, giving it the external semblance of some ancient man-o'-war's hull. It was built by Gilbert Balfour of Westray, between 1560 and 1573, but never completed. Here some of Montrose's officers found refuge after his last defeat in 1650.

Situation. At Pierowall.

Admission. All reasonable times without charge, on application to custodian.

Official Guide Pamphlet. 3*d.*

Pierowall Church

A ruin consisting of nave and chancel, the latter canted. There are some finely lettered tombstones.

Situation. At Pierowall.

Admission. All times without charge.

Westside (Tuquoy Church)

A twelfth century church, with nave and chancel, the former lengthened in the later Middle Ages. The chancel has a Romanesque arch and was vaulted.

Situation. Bay of Tuquoy.

Admission. All times without charge.

ISLAND OF PAPA WESTRAY

Knap of Howar, Papa Westray

The ruins of two stone structures lying side by side, apparently of a domestic character, recently uncovered by excavation. The character of the masonry suggests parallels with the secondary buildings at the Broch of Gurness.

Situation. West side of island of Papa Westray, near Holland House.

Admission. All times without charge.

HOLM OF PAPA WESTRAY

Chambered Cairn

A megalithic chambered cairn of Neolithic date (*c.* 2000 B.C.). The long narrow chamber is divided into three sub-divisions by transverse walls, while 14 beehive cells open off the walls. Engravings occur—rare examples of megalithic art in Scotland.

Admission. All reasonable times without charge, on application to custodian, Mr. Rendall, Holland, Papa Westray.

ISLAND OF WYRE

Cobbie Row's Castle

This remote structure is probably the earliest stone castle authenticated in Scotland. The *Orkneyinga Saga* tells how about 1145 Kolbein Hruga built a fine stone castle (*steinkastala*) in Wyre. His name, in a corrupted form, is still attached to the present ruins, and as careful excavation has failed to yield traces of any earlier structure, there can be little doubt that the existing remains represent the *steinkastala*. It consists of a small rectangular tower, enclosed in a circular ditch, and associated with later buildings.

Situation. In the centre of the island.

Admission. All times without charge.

St. Mary's Chapel

In a graveyard near the middle of the island of Wyre is a ruinous chapel of the late twelfth century said to have been dedicated to St. Mary although commonly attributed to St. Peter. It is a small rectangular Romanesque structure of nave and chancel. The walls are built of local whinstone. The entrance is in the centre of the west gable through a semi-circular archway. The entrance to the chancel is similar.

Situation. Near Cobbie Row's Castle.

Admission. All times without charge.

PEEBLESHIRE

Peebles: Cross Kirk

The remains of a Trinitarian Friary, consisting of the nave and west tower. The foundations of the claustral buildings, which were on the north side of the nave, have been laid bare.

Situation. In Peebles.

Hours of Admission. Standard. Without charge. Key from custodian in nearby house.

PERTHSHIRE

Abernethy Round Tower

One of the two remaining Irish round towers in Scotland (see also BRECHIN, ANGUS). It dates from about the end of the eleventh century, and the belfry windows are of Romanesque character. Beside it is preserved a Pictish symbol stone.

Situation. In Abernethy.

Admission. All reasonable times without charge on application to custodian.

Dunblane Cathedral

One of Scotland's noblest medieval churches. The existing building dates mainly from the thirteenth century, but embodies a square tower, once free-standing, the lower part of which is Norman work. The cathedral consists of an aisled nave, an aisleless choir, and a lady-chapel attached to the north wall of the choir. There are no transepts. The nave was unroofed after the Reformation, but the whole building was restored in 1892-5, under the direction of Sir Rowand Anderson. Apart from the Norman tower, the oldest portion is the Lady chapel. The east and west gables of the church, and the nave arcade, are particularly fine essays in the high style of the thirteenth century. The church contains some good monuments, also important remnants of the medieval carved oaken stalls. In the nave are buried James IV's mistress, Margaret Drummond, and her two sisters, all poisoned at Drummond Castle in 1502. The cathedral occupies a commanding and beautiful position overlooking the Water of Allan. It is well seen from the railway. The most celebrated Bishop of Dunblane was the saintly Robert Leighton (1661-71).

Situation. In Dunblane.

Admission. Standard (except Sundays in Summer when 2 p.m. to 5.30 p.m.). Without charge.

Telephone No.: Dunblane 2321.

Dunfallandy Stone

An 8th century Pictish cross-slab with a cross, beasts and angels on one side, and with a horseman, seated figures, and Pictish symbols on the other. The one originally stood near Killiecrankie.

Situation. Behind Dunfallandy Cottage, 2 miles S.S.E. of Pitlochry.
Admission. All times without charge.

★*Dunkeld Cathedral*

Beautifully situated on the north bank of the Tay, amid lovely Highland scenery, this is the most romantic of the Scottish cathedrals. The choir has been restored and is in use as the parish church. The nave and the great north-west tower date from the fifteenth century, and are in the custody of the Ministry of Works. There are interesting early sixteenth century wall paintings in the aisle under the Tower. The choir contains the monument of the "Wolf of Badenoch," and the chapter-house is now the mausoleum of the Dukes of Atholl.

Situation. In Dunkeld.

Hours of Admission. Standard.

Admission Fee. 1*s.*

Official Guide Book. 1*s.*

★*Elcho Castle*

This very fine and picturesque example of a sixteenth century fortified mansion survives intact, roof and all, and is remarkable for its great development of tower-like "jambs" or wings, and for the wrought iron grilles which protect its windows. It is well equipped for firearms and is strongly situated on the edge of the quarry from which it was built. A predecessor, at or near the same site, was a favourite lurking place of Wallace. The castle is an ancestral seat of the Earls of Wemyss.

Situation. On the south bank of the Tay, south-east of Perth.

Hours of Admission. Standard.

Admission Fee. 6*d.*

Telephone No.: Perth 3437.

Fowlis Wester: Sculptured Stone

A fine cross-slab, 10 feet high, with Pictish symbols, figure and animal sculpture, and Celtic enrichment. The cross is unique in that its arms extend beyond the slab.

Situation. At Fowlis Wester 6 miles north-east of Crieff.

Admission. All times without charge.

Grandtully: St. Mary's Church

A sixteenth century church, close to Grandtully Castle, remarkable for its finely painted wooden ceiling, with heraldic and symbolic subjects.

Situation. 3 miles east-north-east of Aberfeldy.

Admission. All times without charge, on application to custodian.

**Huntingtower, or Ruthven Castle*

A very fine castellated mansion of the fifteenth and sixteenth centuries beautifully situated on a steep bank overlooking the Almond. It is remarkable by reason of its well-preserved painted ceilings. The ancient seat of the Ruthvens, Earls of Gowrie, it became famous in 1582 as the scene of the "Raid of Ruthven," when the young King James VI was kidnapped by the Earls of Mar and Gowrie.

Situation. 2 miles west of Perth on the Perth-Crieff Road.

Hours of Admission. Standard.

Admission Fee. 6d.

Official Guide Book. 1*s.*

**Inchmahome Priory*

This beautifully situated monastic house, on an island in the Lake of Menteith, is famous as the retreat of the infant Mary Queen of Scots. It was an Augustinian house, founded by Walter Comyn, Earl of Menteith, in 1238. Considerable parts of the church and claustral buildings remain, including much fine work of the thirteenth century. The recumbent monuments of Walter Stewart, first Earl of Menteith and his Countess still survive, as well as that of Sir John Drummond, a fifteenth century benefactor. Remains of the monastic gardens are still traceable.

Situation. On an island in the Lake of Menteith, in south-western Perthshire, 3¾ miles south-east of Aberfoyle.

Access. By ferry from Port of Menteith.

Hours of Admission. April-Sept., Standard. Oct.-March, Standard when weather conditions permit.

Admission Fee. 1*s.* 6*d.*, including ferry to the Island.

Official Guide Pamphlet. 2*d.*

**Meigle: Sculptured Stones* (Plate 11)

Housed in a museum here, is a magnificent collection of 25 sculptured monuments of the Celtic Christian period, all found at or near the old churchyard. Many of these monuments are of the highest artistic and symbolic interest, and the whole collection forms one of the most notable assemblages of Dark Age sculpture in Western Europe.

Situation. In Meigle.

Hours of Admission. Standard; but closed on Sundays.

Admission Fee. 6d.

Official Guide Pamphlet. 3*d.* The Guide Book to Early Christian and Pictish Monuments is also available. Price 5*s.*

Muthill Old Church and Tower

The very interesting ruins of an important medieval parish church, about three miles south of Crieff. At its west end, embedded in the nave, is a tall Norman tower, with good architectural detail. It was once free-standing, like the tower at Dunblane Cathedral. The nave and chancel belong mostly to the early fifteenth century, but the sedilia and some other details are of First Pointed character. There was a Culdee settlement here, and the tall free-standing tower partakes somewhat of a Celtic character.

Situation. In Muthill, 3 miles south of Crieff.

Admission. All times without charge.

Tullibardine Chapel

This is one of the few Collegiate Churches in Scotland which was entirely finished and still remains unaltered. It was founded by Sir David Murray of Dumbarton, ancestor of the Duke of Atholl, in 1446. It is cruciform in plan and has a small western tower entering from the church by a narrow doorway. Each part of the church is of equal size. There is good moulded detail round the internal and external openings. The gable ends are finished with the typical Scottish crow-step of the domestic tradition.

Situation. 6 miles south-east of Crieff off the main Crieff-Auchterarder road.

Admission. All reasonable times without charge, on application to the key-holder, Mr. Maxtone, Tullibardine House by Auchterarder.

RENFREWSHIRE

Barochan Cross, Houston

A fine, free-standing Celtic cross, 11 feet high, with figure sculpture. Not on its original site.

Situation. At Houston, 6 miles north-west of Paisley.

Admission. All times without charge.

Castle Semple Collegiate Church

The church is a rectangular structure with an apsidal east end. A square tower projects from the west gable. The style of the east end is remarkable. The apse is three-sided, each side having three windows of debased Gothic form. An ornate monument in memory of John Lord Semple, killed at Flodden, 1513, is in the north wall at the east end. It reveals the last expiring effort of the Gothic decorative spirit.

Situation. 3 miles west of Howwood.

Admission. Not yet open to the public. May be closely viewed from the outside.

★Newark Castle

A large and fine turreted mansion of the Maxwells, still almost entire. It dates mostly from the sixteenth and seventeenth centuries, but embodies an earlier tower-house. The mansion forms three sides of a square.

Situation. In Port Glasgow.

Hours of Admission. Standard.

Admission Fee. 6*d.*

ROSS AND CROMARTY

Callanish Standing Stones

A cruciform setting of megaliths unique in Scotland and outstanding in Great Britain. The complex comprises an avenue, 27 feet wide, of nineteen standing stones, and 270 feet long terminating in a circle 37 feet in diameter, of thirteen standing stones from which extend on either side a cross row of four stones and beyond a shorter avenue, 12 feet wide of six stones. Associated are two cairns, one lying within the circle and one touching it. The scheme was probably not a single conception but carried out in a series of additions. Other groups of stone circles are in the near vicinity.

Situation. On the island of Lewis; on the ridge of a promontory extending into Loch Roag about 12 miles west of Stornoway, 1¾ miles north-west of Gress Lodge, Back.

Admission. All times without charge.

Dun Carloway Broch

One of the best preserved Iron Age broch towers in the Western Isles. Still standing about 30 feet high.

Situation. On the island of Lewis; 1½ miles south of Carloway about 16 miles north-west of Stornoway.

Admission. All times without charge.

Fortrose Cathedral and Precincts

The existing portions of the cathedral are the south aisle of the nave and the nearby sacristy or undercroft of the chapter-house. Such portions of the cathedral as exist are complete, including the vaulting overhead, and there is much fine detail to be seen of fourteenth century date. The undercroft of the chapter-house is probably earlier; mid-thirteenth century.

Situation. In Fortrose.

Admission. All reasonable times without charge, on application to custodian.

"Steinacleit" Chambered Cairn and Stone Circle

The fragmentary remains of a chambered cairn of Neolithic date (*c.* 2000 B.C.).

Situation. On the island of Lewis, on the south end of Loch an Duin, Shader, north-west of Stornoway.

Admission. All times without charge.

ROXBURGHSHIRE

★*Hermitage Castle* (Plate 22.)

This vast and eerie ruin, standing amid lonely and barren hills, was the ancient stronghold of the de Soulis family, and later of the Douglases. Its history is associated with many stirring and some cruel incidents. The castle has been much added to and altered at various times, and was extensively restored in the early nineteenth century, so that its architectural history is obscure: but the oldest work seems to date from the fourteenth century. Here, in October 1566, Queen Mary visited her wounded lover, Bothwell.

Situation. In Liddesdale, 5½ miles north-east of Newcastleton, off the Hawick-Newcastleton road.

Hours of Admission. Standard.

Admission Fee. 6*d.*

Official Guide Book. 1*s.*

★*Jedburgh Abbey*

A house of Augustinian canons regular, and one of the four famous Border monasteries founded by David I. The remains of the church are mostly Norman or Transitional, and present some remarkable features, notably in the arcading of the choir, an obvious reminiscence of the underslung triforium of Oxford Cathedral. Jedburgh possesses the only complete, or nearly complete, Transitional west front in Scotland. Interesting remnants of the claustral buildings have been uncovered. There is a small museum, including many carved fragments of medieval work and some important monuments of the Anglian period.

Situation. In Jedburgh.

Hours of Admission. Standard.

Admission Fee. 1*s.*

Card Guide. 2*d.*

★*Kelso Abbey*

Another of David I's great foundations, this time for monks of the Tironensian Order. Little but the abbey church remains, and that only in imposing fragments: but the building, which is almost wholly of Norman and Transitional work, is unique in Scotland because the plan has had western as well as eastern transepts, with a tower over both the crossings. This i s the plan of Ely and Bury St. Edmunds, and is derived from the Carolingian and Ottonian minsters of the Rhineland. The best preserved portion is the north transept, a superb piece of design.

Situation. In Kelso.

Hours of Admission. Standard, without charge.

★*Melrose Abbey*

Probably the most famous ruin in Scotland, this beautiful Cistercian abbey, founded by David I, was repeatedly wrecked in the Wars of Independence, notably by Richard II, in 1385. Most of the surviving remains belong to the fifteenth century reconstruction, and represent the finest flowering of Scottish Decorated work. Much of the tracery is obviously derived from York, and probably was designed to fit glass imported thence. The beauty of the figure sculpture associated with the church is unrivalled in Scotland. Much progress has been made in laying bare the foundations of the claustral buildings, which were on the north side of the nave. The Commendator's House, an interesting structure, has been fitted up to form a most attractive museum. Melrose Abbey owes much of its modern fame to the glamour that has been shed around it by the genius of Sir Walter Scott. Somewhere in the church lies buried the heart of Bruce.

Situation. In Melrose.

Hours of Admission. Standard.

Admission Fee. 1s.

Official Guide. 1s.

Telephone No.: Melrose 262.

Smailholm Tower

The tower has an elevated situation on a rocky outcrop commanding a magnificent panoramic view of the Border country. The tower is a simple rectangle, 57 feet high, in a good stage of preservation. It was probably erected in the fifteenth century. The upper part may have been added in the sixteenth century.

Situation. Near Smailholm village, 6 miles north-west of Kelso.

Admission. All reasonable times without charge on application to key-keeper, at Sandyknowe farmhouse.

SHETLAND

Clickhimin Broch

A good example of a broch tower with associated secondary buildings dating to the Iron Age (first centuries B.C.-A.D.).

Situation. Lerwick. About 1 mile south-west of the town.

Admission. All reasonable times without charge, on application to key-keeper.

Official Guide Book. 1s. (Available at Jarlshof).

Fort Charlotte

A fort roughly pentagonal in shape with bastions projecting from each corner. The walls are high and massive and contain gun ports pointing seawards. It is recorded that the fort was begun in 1665 to protect the Sound of Bressay against the Dutch, and that the architect was John Mylne, the King's master mason. In 1673 it was burned with the town of Lerwick by the Dutch, but in 1781 it was repaired. The north and south-west bastions with acute salient angles have the appearance of early seventeenth century work and suggest the existence of a fort previous to that recorded.

Situation. In Lerwick.

Admission. All times without charge.

**Jarlshof*

This is one of the most remarkable archæological sites in Britain. Within the relatively confined space of three acres are exposed the remains of three extensive village settlements occupied from Bronze Age to Viking times. The first major settlement comprising a collection of oval stone-built huts was excellently preserved by windblown sand. At a higher level the massive walls of an Iron Age broch tower and courtyard protect the most perfect examples known of stone-built wheelhouses still partly roofed and dating to the first centuries of our era. Above the sand which mounded over these structures an entire Viking settlement is preserved, the most complete of its kind yet excavated in the British Isles. The seventeenth century "Laird's House" on the crest of the sandy mound is the original of Sir Walter Scott's 'Jarlshof' the home of the fictitious Mr. Mertoun in "The Pirate."

Situation. Sumburgh Head, on the southernmost point of Shetland, close to the Sumburgh airfield. About 22 miles due south of Lerwick. Bus service from Lerwick to Sumburgh.
Hours of Admission. Standard.
Admission Fee. 1*s.*
Official Guide Book. 1*s.* 6*d.*

Mousa Broch

The best preserved example of the remarkable Iron Age broch towers peculiar to Scotland. The tower still stands to a height of over 40 feet all round and is otherwise complete.

Situation. On the island of Mousa, off the east coast of the mainland of Shetland. Access by hire of boat from the village of Sandwick about 14 miles south of Lerwick. Daily bus service between Lerwick and Sandwick.
Admission. All times without charge.
Official Guide Book. 1*s.* (Available at Jarlshof).

Muness Castle

Late 16th century building with oblong central block and circular towers at two of the diagonally opposite corners. The castle is characteristically rubble built, but the treatment of shot holes and other architectural detail is exceptionally fine, recalling Scalloway Castle and the Earl's Palace, Kirkwall.

Situation. On the island of Unst. Access from Lerwick by steamer or overland by bus and ferry.
Admission. All reasonable times without charge on application to keykeeper, Mr. J. Peterson, Castle Cottage, Muness.

Ness of Burgi

A defensive stone-built structure probably of Iron Age date which is related in certain features to the brochs.

Situation. The south-easternmost point of Scatness, South Shetland.
Admission. All times without charge.

★*Scalloway Castle*

A fine castellated mansion on the "two-stepped" plan, built in 1600 by the notorious Patrick Stewart, Earl of Orkney (see also under Kirkwall). The memory of the cruelties inflicted upon his tenantry during its erection is preserved in the tale that blood was mixed with the mortar! Earl Patrick paid for his crimes with his life in 1615.

Situation. In Scalloway, about 6 miles west of Lerwick.
Admission. All reasonable times without charge, on application to custodian.
Official Guide Pamphlet. 3*d.*

Staneydale Temple Site

Neolithic temple, heel-shaped externally, and containing a large oval chamber. In plan the monument is strongly reminiscent of Maltese temples of like date.

Situation. 3½ miles east-north-east of Walls.
Admission. All times without charge.

STIRLINGSHIRE

Antonine Wall and associated works (see p. 55)

Three outstanding lengths of the Antonine Wall, and one wall-fort, are in the custody of the Ministry. These are (from east to west):—

1. *Watling Lodge.* Visible remains of the rampart have been destroyed by agriculture, but the profile of the ditch retains its original V-section.

Situation. 1¼ miles west of Falkirk.

2. *Rough Castle, Roman fort and adjacent length of rampart and ditch.* Rough Castle fort, one of the most notable Roman military sites in Britain, was excavated by the Society of Antiquaries of Scotland in 1903. It has recently been placed in the custody of the Ministry. A programme of archaeological excavation as a preliminary to consolidation is at present (1960) being carried out. The fort covers about an acre, with double ditches, and an annexe on the east side. Several buildings in the fort, and the bath-house in the annexe, were uncovered in 1903, but their plans cannot now be distinguished on the ground. A unique feature is the series of defensive pits, *lilia*, outside the Antonine ditch on the left front of the fort. Two inscriptions identify the garrison, the 6th Nervian cohort. The site of the fort is a most commanding one, on the brink of a ravine in which descends the Rowan Burn.

Situation. 1 mile east of Bonnybridge.

3. *Seabegs Wood.* A good length of rampart and ditch.

Situation. ½ mile west of Bonnybridge.

Admission. All times without charge.

Cambuskenneth Abbey

One of the most famous of Scottish monastic houses, and the scene of Bruce's important Parliament in 1326. Here James III and his Queen are buried. The abbey was founded in 1147 by David I as a house of Augustinian Canons regular. The fine detached tower survives complete, but of the church and conventual buildings little save the foundations is now to be seen. The abbey is beautifully situated on the links of the Forth.

Situation. 1 mile east of Stirling.

Admission. All reasonable times without charge on application to the key-keeper, Mrs. M. Wilson, Alexandra Cottage, 28 South Street, Cambuskenneth.

Official Guide Pamphlet. 3*d.* (Available at Stirling Castle).

★*Stirling Castle*

"Stirling, like a huge brooch, clasps Highlands and Lowlands together." Its royal castle on the great basalt rock, 250 feet high, was thus the strategic centre of Scotland, and looks down upon most of the great formative battle fields of Scottish history. As a fortress and a royal palace, its buildings were frequently destroyed and rebuilt, or refashioned at the whim of monarchs. The wonder is that so much of interest survives, including the fine fifteenth century hall, built by James III; the royal palace mostly the work of James V, and showing a quaint mixture of Gothic with Renaissance details; the Chapel Royal, built by James VI for the christening of Prince Henry in 1594; the fine gatehouse of James IV; and important bastioned outworks dating from the sixteenth, seventeenth and eighteenth centuries. The castle is still in military occupation, so that only parts of it are open to visitors.

Hours of Admission. Standard weekdays: Sundays, Summer 1-7 p.m., Winter, 1-4 p.m.

Admission Fee. 1s.

Official Guide Book. 1s. 6d.

Telephone No.: Stirling 60.

Stirling: The Old Bridge

Erected between 1410 and 1415, this fine bridge consists of four arches. The southern one was rebuilt in 1749, after the original arch had been blown up during the Forty-five to prevent the Highlanders entering the town.

Situation. In Stirling.

Admission. All times without charge.

Stirling: Mar's Wark

A quaint Renaissance mansion with an ornate gatehouse, enriched with sculptures, heraldic bearings, and humorous rhyming inscriptions. It was built by the Regent Mar in 1570.

Situation. At the top of Castle Wynd, Stirling.

Admission. All times without charge.

Stirling: The Argyll Lodging

A great mansion erected about the year 1630; purchased in 1655 by the first Marquess of Argyll. The house has been in use as a military hospital since the later eighteenth century. In scale and architectural character, it is the most impressive town mansion in Scotland of its period. Famous personages associated with it include King Charles II, James VII and the Duke of Cumberland.

Situation. At the top of Castle Wynd, Stirling.

Admission. Not open to the public. In use as a military hospital. May be closely viewed from the outside.

Stirling: The "King's Knot"

A "knot" garden constructed in the King's Park below the Royal Palace of Stirling. It was one of the earliest ornamental gardens in Scotland and was devised with a layout of lawns and terraces with earthen mounds and ramps.

Situation. Below the castle rock on the west side. Clearly visible from the castle ramparts.

Admission. All times without charge.

Westquarter Dovecot

A rectangular type of dovecot of considerable architectural merit. Over the entrance doorway is an heraldic panel dated 1647 containing the arms of Sir William Livingstone of Westquarter. The shield carries quarterly the arms of Livingstone and Callender. Besides the initials of William Livingstone are those of his wife "D" (for dame) "H." "L."

Situation. In Westquarter near Laurieston.

Admission. May be closely viewed from the outside.

WEST LOTHIAN

★*Blackness Castle*

At one time one of the most important fortresses in Scotland; used in the seventeenth century as a prison for Covenanters. It comprises a strong, oblong tower, with a circular staircase tower at the north-east angle probably added at a later date. The tower is well-preserved although much altered, and dates from the fifteenth century.

Situation. 4 miles north of Linlithgow; off the Linlithgow-Queensferry road.

Hours of Admission. Standard.

Admission Fee. 1*s.*

★*Cairnpapple Hill: Sanctuary and Burial Cairns* (Plate 8.)

Originally a Neolithic sanctuary remodelled in the Early Bronze Age (*c.* 1800 B.C.) as a monumental open air temple in the form of a stone circle with enclosing ditch; later (*c.* 1500 B.C.) despoiled and built over by a Bronze Age cairn, considerably enlarged several centuries later: recently excavated and laid out.

Situation. About 1½ miles east of Torpichen and 3 miles north of Bathgate.

Admission. April-September, Standard. In winter by arrangement with custodian at Torpichen Preceptory.

Admission Fee. 6*d.*

Official Guide Pamphlet. 3*d.*

Hunter's Craig or Eagle Rock, Cramond

A natural rock with very much defaced carving said to represent an eagle, and to be of Roman date.

Situation. On the foreshore of the Firth of Forth about ¼ mile west of Cramond.

Admission. All times without charge.

Kinneil House (Plate 24.)

The part under guardianship contains important mural and ceiling decorations, of two dates, the earlier executed for the Regent Arran. In one room is the history of the Good Samaritan drawn in the manner of large cartoons for tapestry design: sixteenth and seventeenth centuries.

Situation. In Bo'ness.

Hours of Admission:	*Weekdays*	*Sundays*
April to September ..	10 a.m. to 7 p.m.	2 p.m. to 7 p.m.
October to March	12 noon to 4 p.m.	2 p.m. to 4 p.m.

Admission Fee. 6*d.*

★*Linlithgow Palace*

"Of all the palaces so fair,
Built for the royal dwelling,
In Scotland, far beyond compare
Linlithgow is excelling."

This noble ruin, burnt by Hawley's Dragoons in 1746, stands beautifully on a green brow overlooking Linlithgow Loch. Of Edward Ist's famous Peel nothing now remains, and the oldest part of the existing pile dates from soon after 1400. The Palace reached its final form in the reign of James V, whose work shows the quaint mixture of Gothic and Renaissance detail characteristic of that reign: but the north wing of the Palace was reconstructed, in the then fashionable neo-classical style, between 1618 and 1633. The architecture of all periods is marked by exceptional richness and beauty. Close to the Palace stands the Parish Church of St. Michael, a fine fifteenth century building, still in use, and not under the Ministry's guardianship.

Situation. In Linlithgow.

Hours of Admission. Standard.

Admission Fee. 1*s.*

Official Guide Book. 1*s.* 6*d.*

Telephone No.: Linlithgow 65.

★*Torpichen Preceptory*

This was the principal Scottish seat of the Knights Hospitallers, or Knights of St. John. The central tower and transepts of their church remain, and show the castellated or martial style of ecclesiastical architecture prevalent in Scotland in the fifteenth century. The west tower arch is of Romanesque date: the nave, now the parish church, was rebuilt in the seventeenth century.

Situation. 2¼ miles north of Bathgate.

Hours of Admission. Standard.

Admission Fee. 6*d.*

Note: Custodian is also custodian of Cairnpapple Hill.

WIGTOWNSHIRE

Barsalloch Fort

The fort is formed by a deep ditch with a mound on each side; in horseshoe form. The ditch measures 33 feet in width by 12 feet in depth.

Situation. On the edge of an eminence 60 feet or 70 feet above the shore at Barsalloch Point, ¾ mile west of Monreith.

Admission. All times without charge.

Big Balcraig and Clachan

Two groups of cup-and-ring scribings of Bronze Age date carved on the natural rock.

Situation. 3 miles east of Port William near the farm of Big Balcraig.

Admission. All times without charge.

Castle of Park, Glenluce

This tall and imposing castellated mansion, still entire, was built, according to an inscription on its walls, by Thomas Hay of Park in 1590. It occupies a conspicuous position on the brow of a hill looking down upon Glenluce. Its builder was a son of the last Abbot of Glenluce.

Situation. ¾ of a mile west of Glenluce.

Admission. Not yet open to the public; may be closely viewed from the outside.

Chapel Finian

A small chapel or oratory probably of tenth-eleventh century date set within a sub-rectangular enclosure of about 50 foot wide. The chapel is rectangular in plan and only the foundations and lower walls remain. In general appearance the building suggests comparisons with the small early chapels found in all Celtic lands and notably in Ireland.

Situation. 5 miles north-west of Port William on the main Glenluce-Port William Road.

Admission. All times without charge.

Druchtag Motehill

The earthwork mound of a Norman castle, with some traces of stone buildings.

Situation. At Mochrum village.

Admission. All times without charge.

Drumtroddan

A group of cup-and-ring markings on a natural rock face of Bronze Age date, and 400 yds. to the south an alignment of three adjacent surviving stones, two upright and one now fallen.

Situation. 2 miles north-east of Port William. On the Glenluce-Whithorn Road.

Admission. All times without charge.

★Glenluce Abbey

A Cistercian house founded in 1190 by Roland, Earl of Galloway. The ruins occupy a site of great beauty and are in themselves of much architectural distinction and interest. The abbey church is in the First Pointed style, and there is a fine vaulted chapter-house, dating from the later fifteenth century. Of the church, the south aisle and the south transept are the principal remains. There are some interesting tombstones.

Situation. 2 miles north-west of Glenluce village.

Hours of Admission. Standard.

Admission Fee. 6*d.*

Kirkmadrine: Early Christian Stones

At this lonely church are three of the earliest Christian monuments in Britain, showing the Chi-Rho symbol and inscriptions dating from the fifth or early sixth century.

Situation. In the Rhinns of Galloway, 2 miles south-west of Sandhead.

Admission. All times without charge.

Official Guide Book. See under Whithorn Priory.

Laggangairn Standing Stones

Two flat slabs marked with re-duplicated incised crosses of an early pattern

Situation. At Killgallioch, parish of New Luce.

Admission. All times without charge.

Monreith Cross

A notable free-standing wheel-headed cross with interlaced enrichment, 7 feet 6 inches high.

Situation. In the grounds of Monreith House, at Monreith, near Port William.

Admission. All reasonable times without charge.

Rispain Camp

A rectangular enclosure defined by double banks and ditches. Probably of Iron Age date; unexcavated.

Situation. 1 mile west of Whithorn near Rispain Farm.

Admission. All times without charge.

St. Ninian's Cave

This cave is traditionally associated with the Saint who established the first Christian Church in Scotland in the early fifth century. It might well have been his place of retreat, as within there has been found a fine assemblage of early Christian crosses, now displayed in the museum attached to Whithorn Priory. Both upon the walls of the cave and the rocks outside Christian crosses have been incised at an early date and may be seen in situ behind protective grilles.

Situation. Physgill; on the coast 4 miles south-west of Whithorn. Footpath from Kidsdale Farm.

Admission. All times without charge.

Official Guide Book. Described in Whithorn Priory Guide Book, 1*s.* 6*d.*

St. Ninian's Chapel

The ruins of a chapel of thirteenth century date, alleged by some to be on the site of St. Ninian's first settlement in Scotland. Recent excavations have, however, failed to produce evidence of an earlier church. (See Whithorn Priory). The chapel is a simple rectangle on plan. It had a doorway in the south wall, a pointed arched window in the north wall and a larger arched window in the east wall. The exterior is quite plain. The chapel stood within an enclosing wall, of which evidence is still visible.

On the point of the promontory may be seen the earthworks of an Iron Age fort.

Situation. The Isle of Whithorn, about 5 miles from Whithorn.

Admission. All times without charge.

Official Guide Book. Described in Whithorn Priory Guide Book, 1*s.* 6*d.*

Torhouse Stone Circle

A circle of 19 boulders standing on the edge of a low mound. Probably Bronze Age in date.

Situation. About 4 miles west of Wigtown and some 700 yards south-east of Torhousekie farm.

Admission. All times without charge.

★Whithorn Priory

A monastery at Whithorn was founded by St. Ninian in the early fifth century, and here he built his *Candida Casa*, or "White House," dedicated to St. Martin. This was the first Christian church in Scotland. The priory was founded by Fergus, Lord of Galloway, in the twelfth century, for Premonstratensian canons regular. Soon afterwards it became the cathedral church of Galloway. The ruins are scanty, but the chief feature of interest is the fine Norman doorway of the nave. In the museum are preserved a notable group of early Christian monuments, including the Latinus stone, dating from the fifth century, and the St. Peter Stone, showing a late form of the Chrism or Chi-Rho monogram.

Recent excavations at the priory church indicate that the foundations of a small building which projects from under the east end are the remnants of the church founded by the Saint in the early fifth century. (See St. Ninian's Chapel).

Situation. At Whithorn.

Hours of Admission. Standard.

Admission Fee. *6d.*

Official Guide Book. *1s. 6d.* The Guide Book to Early Christian and Pictish Monuments of Scotland is also available. Price *5s.*

The "Wren's Egg" Stone Circle

The remains of a standing stone circle, originally a double concentric ring. Only three stones remain, including the central one.

Situation. 2 miles south-east of Port William near the farmhouse of Blairbuy.

Admission. All times without charge.

BIBLIOGRAPHY

General

Full descriptions of the monuments in the counties of Berwickshire; Caithness; Dumfries; East Lothian; Fife; Kinross and Clackmannan; Galloway, vol. I: Wigtown, vol. II; Kirkcudbright; Midlothian and West Lothian; Orkney and Shetland; Roxburgh; Selkirkshire; Skye; Hebrides and Small Isles; Sutherland, and the City of Edinburgh, will be found in the Inventories published under these titles by the Royal Commission on Ancient and Historical Monuments, Scotland.

ALLEN, J. ROMILLY. "Early Christian Monuments of Scotland." 1903.
ANDERSON, JOSEPH. "Scotland in Early Christian Times." (2 vols.) 1881.
HANNAH, I. C. "The Story of Scotland in Stone." 1934.
MACGIBBON and ROSS. "Castellated and Domestic Architecture of Scotland." (5 vols.) 1887-1892.
"Ecclesiastical Architecture of Scotland" (3 vols.). 1896-1897.
MAXWELL, Sir JOHN STIRLING, "Shrines and Homes of Scotland." 1937.
SIMPSON, W. DOUGLAS. "The Province of Mar." 1943. "The Earldom of Mar." 1949.
"The Stones of Scotland," a Batsford book by five leading authorities: edited by G. SCOTT-MONCRIEFF. 1938.

Prehistoric Periods

CHILDE, V. G. "The Prehistory of Scotland." 1934. "Scotland Before the Scots." 1946.
"The Problem of the Picts," by five leading authorities. Edited by F. T. WAINWRIGHT. 1955.

Roman Period

CRAWFORD, O. G. S. "The Topography of Roman Scotland," 1949.
MCDONALD, G. "The Roman Wall in Scotland." 1934.
ORDNANCE SURVEY. Map of "Roman Britain."

Post-Roman Periods

CHADWICK, H. M. "Early Scotland." 1949.
CRUDEN, STEWART. "Early Christian and Pictish Monuments." H.M.S.O. 1957.
"Scottish Abbeys," H.M.S.O., 1960.
"The Scottish Castle," 1960.
MACKENZIE, W. MACKAY. "The Medieval Castle in Scotland." 1927.
SKENE, W. F. "Celtic Scotland" (3 vols.) 1886; for historical review of the early Christian period.
SIMPSON, W. DOUGLAS. "The Celtic Church in Scotland." 1935. "St. Ninian and Christian Origins in Scotland." 1940. "Scottish Castles." H.M.S.O. 1959.
ORDNANCE SURVEY. Maps of "Monastic Britain," north sheet; and "Britain in the Dark Ages."

Excavation reports, detailed papers on individual monuments and various aspects of Scottish archæology will be found in the Proceedings of the Society of Antiquaries of Scotland and other similar bodies.

INDEX

First figures refer to text, second to the "Notes."

Ancient Monuments and Historic Buildings

Many interesting ancient sites and buildings are maintained as national monuments by the Ministry of Works. Guide-books, postcards, colour transparencies and specially produced photographs are available as follows:

GUIDE-BOOKS or pamphlets are on sale at most monuments, and are also obtainable from the bookshops of H.M. Stationery Office. A complete list of titles and prices is contained in Sectional List No. 27 available free on request from any of the addresses given on page 2.

POSTCARDS and colour transparencies can be purchased at many monuments, or from the Clerk of Stationery, Ministry of Works, 122 George Street, Edinburgh 2 (Clerk of Stationery, Ministry of Works, Lambeth Bridge House, London, S.E.1 for English and Welsh Monuments).

OFFICIAL PHOTOGRAPHS of most monuments may be obtained in large prints (e.g. size $8\frac{1}{2}'' \times 6\frac{1}{2}''$ or $10'' \times 8''$), at commercial rates plus postage, from the Under Secretary, Ministry of Works, 122 George Street, Edinburgh 2 (Photographic Librarian, Ministry of Works, Lambeth Bridge House, London, S.E.1 for English and Welsh Monuments).

Printed in Scotland under the authority of Her Majesty's Stationery Office.
Letterpress by Messrs. Pickering & Inglis Ltd., Glasgow.
Lithographic Map by Messrs. Jas. Deas & Son, Edinburgh

Wt. 73889 K.48

S.O. Code No. 67-9-6-61*